THE STREET BOOK

Edited by Thomas Tracy

Book and Cover Design by Diana Graham

Picture Research by Ann Novotny and
Rosemary Eakins of *Research Reports,* New
York, with the assistance of David Bertugli,
Charles Cooney, Susan Kapsis, and Shari
Segel.

Cover Illustration:
New York City in the mid-19th century,
looking east, south and west from the steeple
of St. Paul's (drawn by J.W. Hill, engraved by
Henry Papprill, published in 1849 by H.I.
Megarey.)

THE STREET BOOK

An Encyclopedia of Manhattan's Street Names and Their Origins

Henry Moscow

FORDHAM UNIVERSITY PRESS

New York

This edition is published by exclusive arrangement with
Macmillan Publishing Company, a division of Maxwell
Macmillan Inc., and with Hagstrom Map Company, Inc.

Fordham University Press edition 1990

10 9 8

Moscow, Henry.
    The Street Book : an encyclopedia of Manhattan's street names and their
origins / Henry Moscow.
    114 p. ill., maps.
    Originally published: 1978.
    ISBN 0–8232–1275–0
    1. Streets—New York (N.Y.) 2. Manhattan (New York, N.Y.)—Streets.
3. Street names—New York (City), I. Title
    F128.67.A1 M6 1990
    917.471M   78-66990

Contents

The landing of Henry Hudson on Manhattan.

Introduction

Most readers of books, I suspect, skip the introductions; you will not be importuned to ingest this one. But if you have become a little vague about what you were taught—or should have been taught—in elementary school, you may find a brief retelling of New York's story helpful in fitting together the pieces of mosaic that make up this book. So . . .

For everyone except American Indians, Manhattan's history began on a day in May of 1524, when the ship *Delfina* poked its bow through The Narrows.

"We found a very pleasant situation amongst some steep hills, through which a very large river, deep at its mouth, forced its way to the sea," the *Delfina's* Florentine skipper, Giovanni da Verrazano, later reported to King Francis I of France, who had financed the voyage. "From the sea to the estuary of the river, any ship, heavily laden, might pass with the help of the tide, which runs eight feet. But as we were riding at anchor in a good berth, we would not venture up in our vessel without a knowledge of the mouth. Therefore, we took the boat, and entering the river, we found the country on its banks well peopled, the inhabitants not differing much from the others [whom he had encountered farther south, probably on the Carolina coast], being dressed out with feathers of birds of different colors. They came toward us with evident delight, raising loud shouts of admiration, and showing us where we could most securely land with our boat. We passed up the river about half a league, where it formed a most beautiful lake, three leagues in circuit, upon which they were rowing thirty or more of their small boats, from one shore to the other, filled with multitudes who came to see us. All of a sudden, as is wont to happen to navigators, a violent contrary wind blew in from the sea, and forced us to return to our ship, greatly regretting to leave the region, which seemed so commodious and delightful, and which we supposed also must contain great riches, as the hills showed many indications of minerals."

King Francis missed the cue and Verrazano never returned to investigate the "great riches." (Verrazano vanished mysteriously on a later voyage; he may have been eaten by South Americans, it is suggested, or hanged as a pirate, for he *had* engaged in privateering.) Shortly after Verrazano's visit, a Portuguese navigator, Ésteban Gomez, also passed this way but did not stay. It was

Official seal of the City of New York.

quite a while before anybody did stay even briefly: not until about 1598 did Dutchmen who worked in summer in Greenland begin to winter here in two small forts that they built. It was a nice place to visit, they seemed to have thought, but they didn't want to live here. Henry Hudson, of course, put the island on the map figuratively—it already was on the map literally—when he sailed up the river that bears his name. The year, as everyone knows, was 1609 and four years later, in 1613, the British skipper Samuel Argall reported having seen four little houses on the island. Their addresses would be 39, 41, 43, and 45 Broadway and they were the shelters, presumably, of the Dutch fur traders, Captains Adriaen Block and Hendrick Christaensen and their crews. Block and Christaensen had been here before, in 1611, and had taken back to Europe two Indians whom they unsuitably named Orson and Valentine. This time, Block's ship *Tyger* had burned at its mooring, where the World Trade Center now stands on filled land. (Some of *Tyger*'s charred timbers were found in 1916, during construction of a subway, and the rest probably lie buried beneath the Trade Center's towers.) So Block was building another vessel, on the site of Fraunces' Tavern. (The new craft, *Onrust,* or *Restless,* was a 16-tonner and, of course, the first ship ever constructed here.) One of the four little houses may have been the birthplace of Manhattan's first white native. He was Jean Vigné, whose parents were Guillaume and Adrienne Cuville Vigné. European travelers who visited him in 1679 estimated his age at about 65, which would have made 1614 the year of his birth. But Vigné may have been ten years younger than his acquaintances guessed, and a first fruit of the 1624 baby crop that impelled an appeal to Amsterdam for a minister because there were infants to baptize. Vigné's name, obviously, is French—which points to a bit of history that the writer never learned in school. When the Dutch West India Company—a consortium of five Dutch cities of which Amsterdam was the first among equals—was authorized in 1623 to settle New Netherland from the South (Delaware) River to the North (Hudson) River, the first colonists it recruited were French-speaking Belgians rather than Dutchmen. The Belgians were the Protestant Walloons, and they were seeking refuge from religious persecution in the Catholic Spanish Netherlands. They were thirty couples and their families, totaling perhaps 110 people, when they sailed from Holland in 1624 in the ship *New Netherland*, Captain Cornelis Jacobsen May commanding. But it was a long voyage, via western Africa: when they arrived here, there were thirty-four couples. May, who had authority as governor, chose eight men to remain on Manhattan and dispersed the rest to such suburbs as Albany, which was dubbed Fort Orange in tribute to the Dutch reigning house. When May sailed home, one Willem ter Hulst took over as governor. But the colonists shipped him out for bad conduct and elected in his stead Ter Hulst's assistant, a brawny, brainy fellow named Peter Minuit— Peter Midnight— who had not planned to stay and had not brought his wife. German by birth because his parents were refugees in Germany when he was born, Belgian by blood, French by name and Dutch by residence, Minuit foreshadowed modern New Yorkers in his energy as well as his complex origins. Elected, he departed for Holland, won appointment by the Dutch West India Company as director-general of New Netherland with full authority, and returned to Manhattan in 1626. He immediately called in the colonists from the sticks and, with the arrival of 45 more Walloons, soon had a village of 200 on the island's southern tip. A stickler for fairness and legality, he assembled Indian chiefs and their squaws— who whispered advice to their husbands— and arranged to purchase the island for cloth and costume jewelry worth 60 guilders, or $24. (The exchange rate is the same today.) He built a crude fort, mills for grain and bark, which was essential for tanning, and shelters.

The island on which Minuit established the town that came to be called New Amsterdam was indeed the "commodious and delightful" place that Verrazano had deemed it. "The sole inhabitants," Mary L. Booth wrote in 1859, "were a tribe of dusky Indians— an offshoot from the great nation of the Lenni Lenape, who inhabited the vast territory bounded by the Penobscot and Potomac, the Atlantic and Mississippi— dwelling in the clusters of rude wigwams that dotted here and there the surface of the country [which] was gently undulating, presenting every variety of hill and dale, of brook and rivulet. The upper part of the island was rocky and covered by dense forest; the lower part grassy, and rich in wild fruits and flowers. Grapes and strawberries grew in abundance in the fields, and nuts of various kinds were plentiful in the forests, which were also filled with abundance of game. The brooks and ponds were swarming with fish, and the soil was of luxurious fertility. In the vicinity of the Tombs [the old city prison] was a deep, clear and beautiful pond of fresh water (with a picturesque little island in the middle)— so deep, indeed, that it could have floated the largest ship in our navy— which was for a long time deemed bottomless by its possessors . . . . Smaller ponds dotted the island in various places, two of which, lying near each other, in the vicinity of the present corner of the Bowery and Grand Street, collected the waters of the high grounds which surrounded them. To

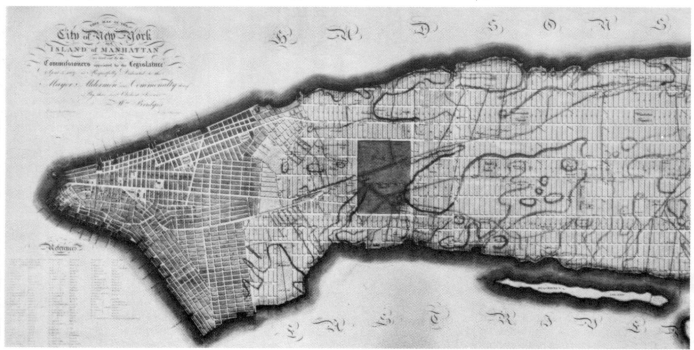

The Randel Survey (or Bridges) map of 1811; line engraving on copper adapted by William Bridges from the original survey by John Randel, Jr.

the north-west of the Fresh Water Pond [later called the Collect, on the site of Foley Square] . . . and extending to the northward over an area of some seventy acres, lay an immense marsh . . . tenanted with frogs and watersnakes. A little rivulet connected this marsh with the Fresh Water Pond, which was also connected—by the stream which formed its outlet—with another strip of marshy land, covering the region now occupied by James, Cherry and the adjacent streets. An unbroken chain of waters was thus stretched across the island from James street at the south-east to Canal street at the north-west. An inlet occupied the place of Broad street, a marsh covered the vicinity of Ferry street, Rutgers street formed the center of another marsh, and a long line of meadows and swampy ground stretched to the northward along the eastern shore.

"The highest line of lands lay along Broadway, from the Battery to the northernmost part of the island, forming its backbone and sloping gradually to the east and west. On the corner of Grand street and Broadway was a high hill, commanding a view of the whole island, and falling off gradually to the Fresh Water Pond . . . ." The hill was part of the Zantberg, a sandy range that ran from what is now Gramercy Park to Charlton and Varick streets.

Minuit enjoyed his idyllic-looking—and mosquito-infested—domain no more than half a dozen years. Like many an executive after him, he had a run-in over policy with the home office, and was fired. (And like Verrazano and Henry Hudson, whose mutinous crew put him off his own ship on Hudson's Bay in 1611, Minuit vanished at sea.) He was succeeded briefly by Jans Sebastian Krol, the colonist who had asked for the minister. Krol gave way to Wouter van Twiller, whose connections in Amsterdam were better than Krol's, and Willem van Kieft replaced van Twiller. Then came Peter Stuyvesant, who ran the town until the British took it from him, without firing a shot, in 1664. The British, who renamed it New York, lost it back to the Dutch in 1673, and this time the Dutch called it New Orange. But the Dutch yielded it again to the British the following year, getting Surinam as their compensation. Once again, the settlement was New York.

Some twenty years before, the Dutch had incorporated the company town as a city. But it had been acting like a city and a future metropolis from virtually the beginning. In 1631, a mere seven years after the colonists stepped ashore, Peter Minuit constructed the biggest ship in the world at the time, an 800-ton vessel which he christened *New Netherland* after the little craft in which the colonists had come. (Though Minuit used the splendid local timber, the vessel encountered vast cost overruns in construction and required an impractically large crew. But it awed Europe after it crossed the Atlantic.)

Father Isaac Jogues, a Jesuit who was later canonized, visited New Amsterdam in 1643 and reported that among its 500 inhabitants 18 languages were spoken. He did not include, probably, the Greek, Latin

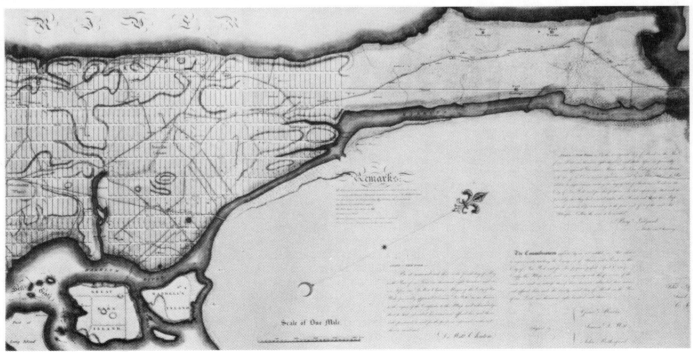

(engraved by P. Maverick).

and Hebrew that were familiar to the college graduates among them. (Anyone who Latinized his name by adding the suffix *us* was proclaiming that he had been thus educated, but some didn't bother.) The Jesuit, who had been brutalized by Indians, was surprised and moved by the welcome he got in the almost entirely Protestant community—he was feasted, feted and decked out in new clothes to replace his rags.

Far from being the stiff-necked dour Dutchmen of tradition, New Amsterdam's folk were for the most part a lively, lusty bunch who had to be reminded constantly and despairingly by their governors that they should not play tennis (yes, tennis), drink and go riding in cars (sic) on Sundays when they ought to be listening to sermons. By 1644,

under Kieft, they even had issued their own Emancipation Proclamation, freeing black slaves who had arrived in 1625 and 1626, and setting them up as independent farmers. A decade later, civil rights and open-housing crusades erupted: Jews who arrived in 1654 wanted to serve in the militia and to buy homes, but Peter Stuyvesant—the only bigot among the Dutch governors—said 'Nay" and attempted to expel them from the colony. But the Jews appealed to Amsterdam, which upheld them and stiffly cautioned Stuyvesant that Dutchmen did not behave that way. (Other New Amsterdammers had helped the Jews financially when they arrived destitute, having been robbed by pirates and cheated by their French rescuer.)

The settlement, in short, had many of the aspects of later New York—including corruption (Van Twiller had appropriated some of the best company-owned lands to himself), financial problems (the Dutch West India Company never made any money out of its venture) and pollution (smelly little factories had to be banished by law to the town's outskirts).

Nor were things more tranquil much of the time under the British. One governor, Jacob Leisler, who had been popularly chosen to serve until the king could send a replacement to fill a vacancy, was framed and hanged for treason in a feud between the Protestant bourgeoisie and the Catholic aristocracy. Another, Lord Cornbury—a father of seven children, an army officer and a cousin of Queen Ann—amused the citizenry by flouncing along Broadway in women's clothes and outraged them by borrowing money that he never repaid. And in the decade before the Revolutionary War, the turmoil of course far exceeded anything that had preceded it. The names of some of those who contributed to that turmoil and helped to bring about American independence—and the names of some of those who fought the very idea—are commemorated in the designations of many Manhattan streets today.

When the British finally abandoned the city in 1783, after having held it throughout the war, it still was a small place extending north only to the site of the present City Hall. But at the turn of the century, it began to burst at its seams. On January 20, 1806, the city council felt it necessary to resolve that "it is highly important that a correct survey and map be made of the Island of New York"—which meant, of course, only Manhattan. And on April 3, 1807, the council appointed Gouverneur Morris, Simeon De Witt and John Rutherford commissioners to design "the leading streets and great avenues, of a width not less than 60 feet, and in general to layout said streets, roads and public squares of such ample width as they may deem sufficient to ensure a free and abundant circulation of air among said streets and public squares when the same shall be built upon."

The commissioners considered a plan of curves and circles like that which characterizes Washington, D.C., but decided that "straight-sided and right-angled houses are the most cheap to build and the most convenient to live in." So what they came up with in 1811, in a map drawn by John Randel, Jr., was a so-called grid plan of rectangular, symmetrical avenues 100 feet wide and streets mostly 60 feet wide, interspersed with occasional public squares. Avenues that could be extended some day north to Harlem

were numbered from First to Twelfth (reading from right to left if one faced uptown). East of First, the avenues that geography would keep short were designated A, B, C, and D. (The plan did not attempt to deal with cross streets that had just grown, in Dutch and British days, along paths, trails, the dividing lines of farms or roads long in use.)

"The map and plan of the Commissioners," ecstasized one critic, "laid out the highways on the island upon so magnificent a scale, and with so bold a hand, and with such prophetic views, in respect to the future growth and extension of the city, that it will form an everlasting monument of the stability and wisdom of the measure." The planners indeed made Manhattan the easiest urban area in the world in which to find one's way. But gone, alas, are the hills and dales, the brooks and rivulets that delighted the eye and the spirit; they were flattened or filled in the execution of the commissioners' plan. Besides, numbers bespeak no history. But enough Manhattan streets do retain names to recall to the informed pas-

serby some scores of the people who helped to make us what we are.

History is biography, Emerson wrote. But biography, in turn, is history and in the following pages much of Manhattan's past is recounted in brief biographical sketches. In linking people's names and street names, the writer has striven for accuracy, but records are scattered, often incomplete and sometimes nonexistent. Where the writer has erred, he will welcome correction for the sake of the city he loves. And he apologizes to Brooklyn, Queens, Staten Island and The Bronx, which were united with Manhattan in Greater New York in 1898, for limiting himself to Manhattan. Their pasts too abound in fascinating stories—too many to be encompassed in one book. After all, those stories have had lots of time in which to accumulate, for William Shakespeare and Queen Elizabeth I and Rembrandt Harmens van Rijn were contemporaries of the folk who got us all started.

Map of New York City after a 1728 survey.

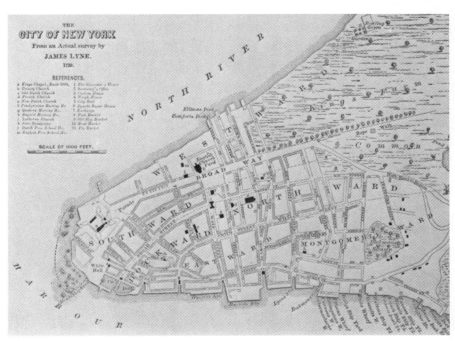

The following maps provide an easy reference for finding streets in Manhattan. We have divided our map into seven overlapping sections. Use the grid system to locate specific streets.

Maps courtesy of Hagstrom Company, Inc.

A5	Admiral George Dewey Promenade
B4	Albany Street
E6	Allen Street
C5	Ann Street
E4	Avenue of the Americas
C6	Avenue of the Finest
C4	Barclay Street
A4	Battery Place
E6	Baxter Street
D6	Bayard Street
D4	Beach Street
B5	Beaver Street
C5	Beekman Street
D5	Benson Street
B5	Bowling Green
A5	Bridge Street
B5	Broad Street
E4	Broome Street
B6	Burling Slip
E4	Canal Street
D6	Cardinal Hayes Place
B4	Carlisle Street
D5	Catherine Lane
D5	Catherine Street
B5	Cedar Street
C4	Centre Street
C5	City Hall Park
D4	Chambers Street
D6	Chatham Square
D7	Cherry Street
E6	Chrystie Street
D5	Church Street
C6	Cliff Street
E6	Clinton Street
B5	Coenties Alley
B5	Coenties Slip
D4	Collister Street
E8	Columbia Street
C5	Cortlandt Street
E5	Crosby Street
B6	Depeyster Street
E3	Desbrosses Street
C5	Dey Street
E7	Division Street
E4	Dominick Street
C6	Dover Street
D6	Doyers Street
D4	Duane Street
C6	Dutch Street
D6	East Broadway
B5	Edgar Street
E6	Eldridge Street
D5	Elk Street
E6	Elizabeth Street
D4	Ericsson Place
E7	Essex Street
B5	Exchange Place
D4	Finn Square
B6	Fletcher Street
D6	Florence Place
D6	Foley Square
E6	Forsyth Street
C6	Frankfort Street
D4	Franklin Street
C6	Franklin Square
B6	Front Street
C5	Fulton Street
C5	Gold Street
B6	Governeur Lane
B6	Governeur Slip
B6	Governeur Street
E4	Grand Street
D4	Greenwich Street
D6	Hamill Place
B5	Hanover Street
B5	Hanover Square
D4	Harrison Street
D6	Harry Howard Square
D6	Henry Street

E6	Hester Street
D6	Howard Street
D4	Hubert Street
D4	Hudson Street
E8	Jackson Street
C6	James Street
D4	Jay Street
A6	Jeanette Park
E7	Jefferson Street
C5	John Street
E6	Kenmare Street
E5	Lafayette Street
D4	Laight Street
D4	Leonard Street
A3	Leroy Street
E8	Lewis Street
B5	Liberty Place
B4	Liberty Street
E5	Lispenard Street
C5	Madison Street
C5	Maiden Lane
B5	Marketfield Street
D7	Market Street
E5	Mercer Street
B6	Mill Lane
D7	Monroe Street
E8	Montgomery Street
B4	Morris Street
E6	Mott Street
D4	Moore Street
E6	Mulberry Street
C4	Murray Street
B5	Nassau Street
B5	New Street
D4	North Moore Street
D6	Oliver Street
E7	Orchard Street
D4	North Moore Street
C4	Park Place
D6	Park Street
B6	Park Row
D6	Pearl Street
B5	Pearl Street
C6	Peck Slip
D6	Pell Street
D7	Pike Street
B6	Pine Street
E7	Pitt Street
B5	Platt Street
B5	Printing House Square
B5	Reade Street
B4	Rector Street
E4	Renwick Street
D6	Robert F. Wagner Sr. Place
D7	Rutgers Street
C6	Saint James Place
E4	Saint Johns Lane
E6	Sara Roosevelt Parkway
E6	Schiff Parkway
B6	South Street
B6	South William Street
E4	Spring Street
C5	Spruce Street
D4	Staple Street
A5	State Street
A5	Stone Street
E4	Sullivan Street
B5	Thames Street
C5	Theatre Alley
D4	Thomas Street
E4	Thompson Street
D5	Trimble Place
B5	Trinity Place
E4	Vandam Street
D4	Varick Street
C4	Vesey Street
E3	Vestry Street
E5	Walker Street
B5	Wall Street

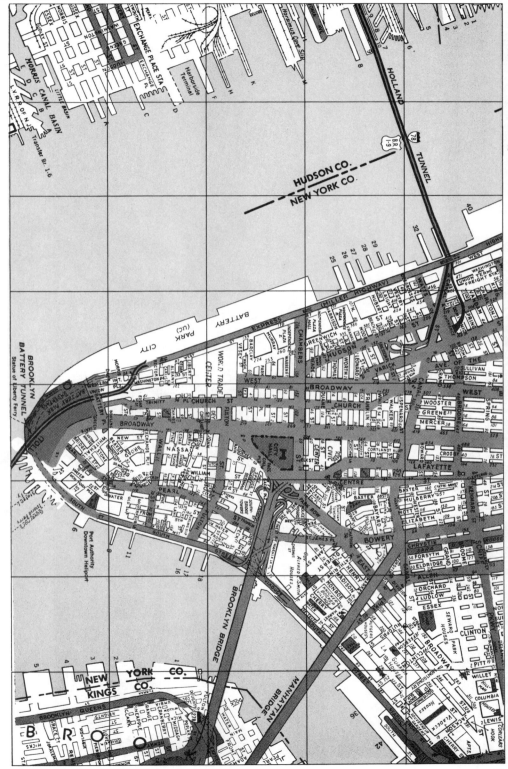

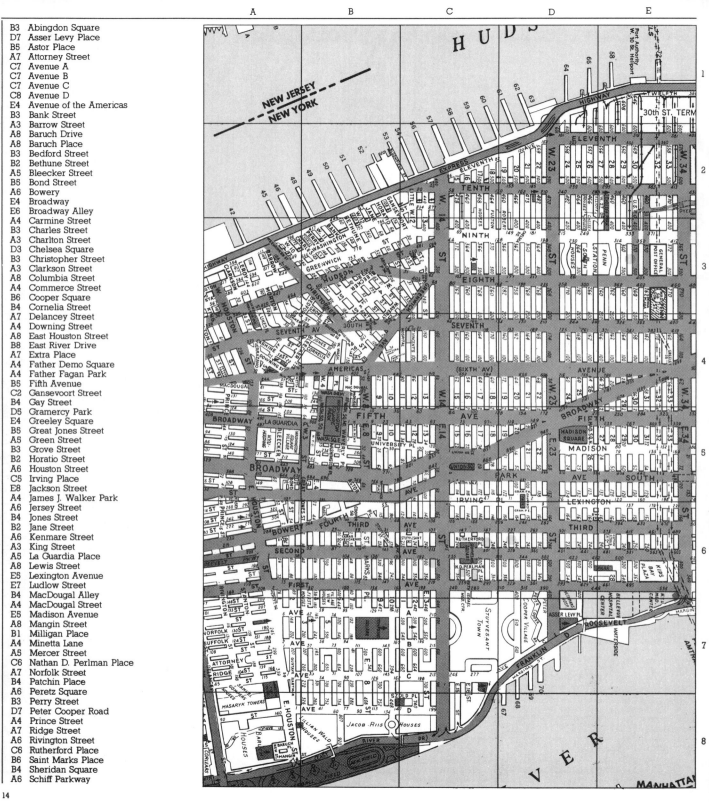

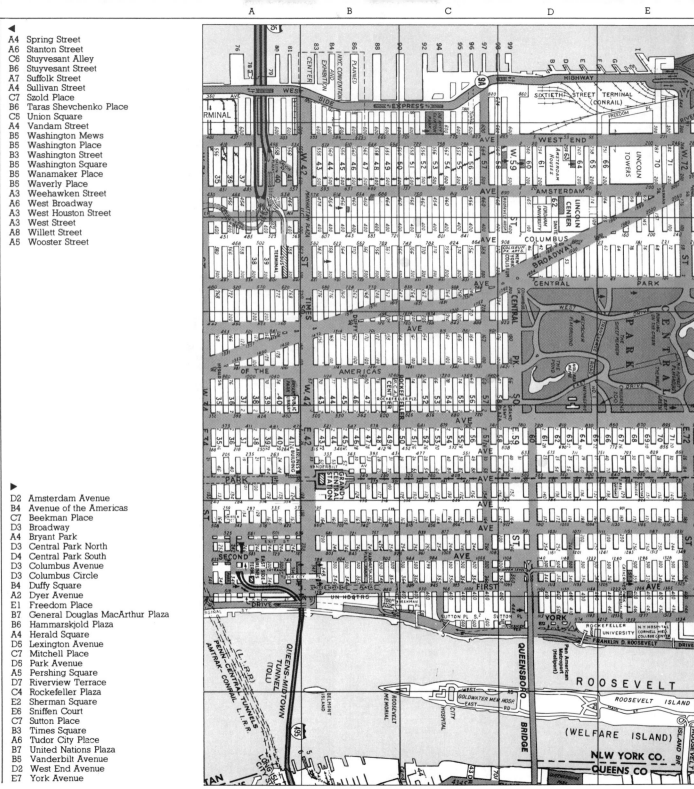

15

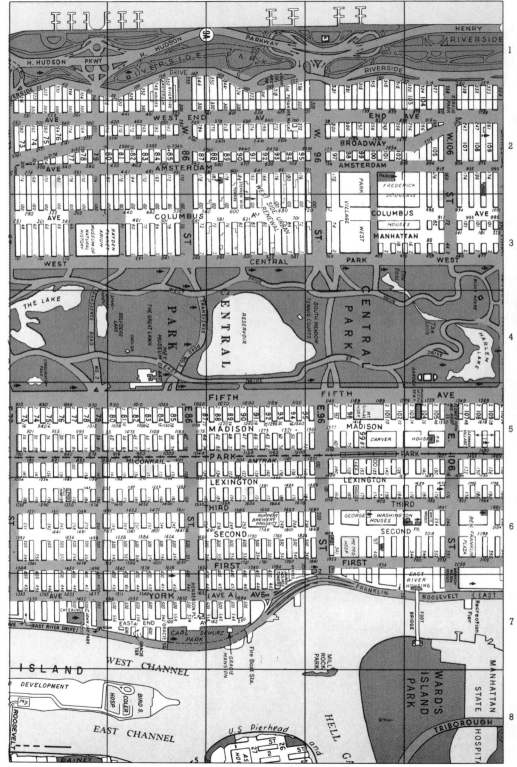

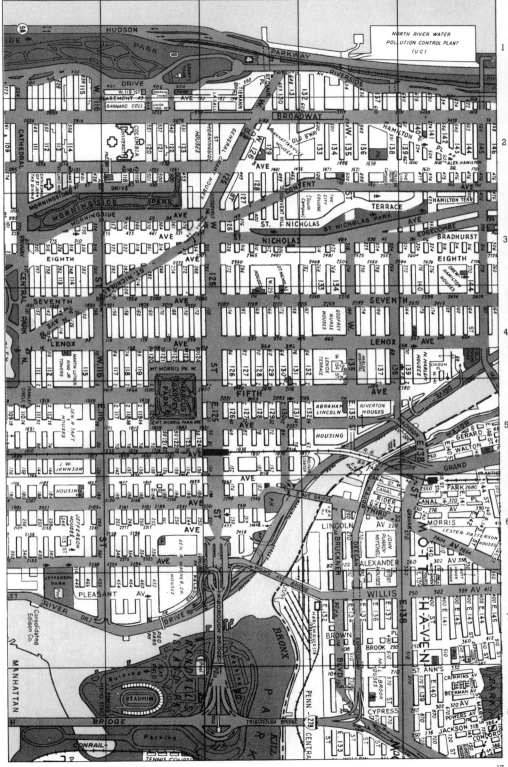

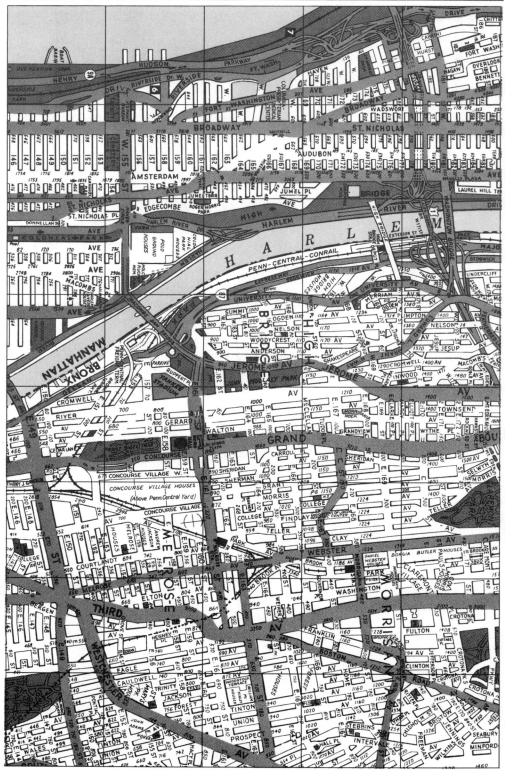

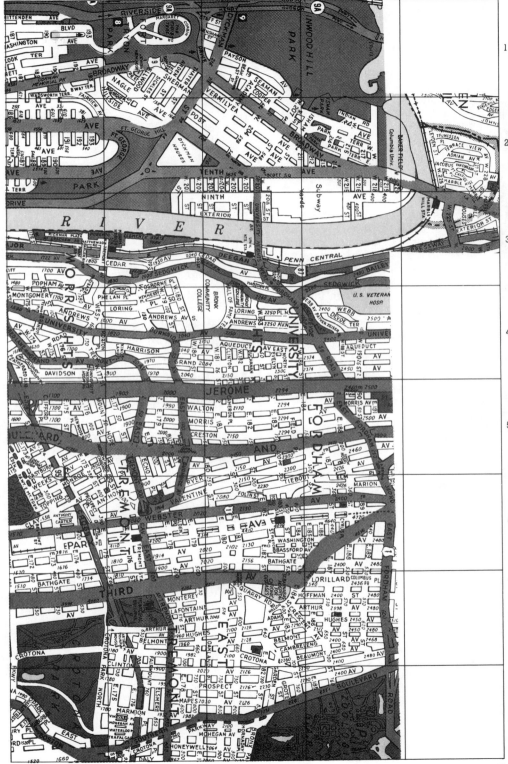

Abingdon Square

The Namesake: Charlotte Warren, a pre-Revolutionary War Greenwich Village belle, who became the bride of the Earl of Abingdon. Her father was Admiral Sir Peter Warren, a naval hero and New York social lion, and her mother was the beautiful and wealthy Susannah de Lancey (*see* Warren Street and Oliver Street).

Charlotte's father bought 300 acres in Greenwich Village in 1744, paying with his loot from his exploits at sea against French and Spanish treasure ships. The admiring city fathers voted him additional land as a gift and named streets for him and his three daughters. The Warrens' mansion stood in the block bounded by Charles, Perry, Bleecker and Tenth streets. In 1794, more than a decade after the end of the Revolution, the city council, acting after all due deliberation, changed the designation of streets and places with British names. But Abingdon Square's name survived because Charlotte and her husband, the Earl, had been friendly to the patriots' cause.

Academy Street

The Namesake: Public School 52.

A Tudor-style building, the school occupied the whole block. The structure, in the Dyckman Street area of northern Manhattan known as Inwood, was pulled down in 1957.

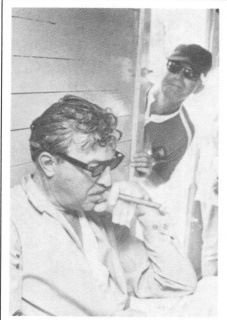

Adam Clayton Powell Jr. Boulevard

The Namesake: the handsome, flamboyant 11-term Representative in Congress from Harlem and swinging pastor of the Abyssinian Baptist Church on West 138th Street. He was first elected to Congress in 1944.

A crusader for civil rights for decades before the Montgomery, Alabama, bus boycott, a powerful spokesman for his fellow blacks and an effective chairman of the House Committee on Education and Labor, Dr. Powell was also a playboy who defied public opinion and legal authority when it pleased him to do so.

Two episodes in particular contributed to his eventual downfall. In 1962, he toured Europe for six weeks at public expense accompanied by the 21-year-old former beauty queen who was the receptionist in his Congressional office, and by the 31-year-old woman counsel to his committee. A little later, he was sued for damages by a woman whom he had named in connection with payoffs to corrupt police; when he lost the case, he refused to pay her the $575,000 that the court awarded. (On appeal, the amount was reduced to $55,787.) Held in civil contempt, Dr. Powell evaded arrest by staying out of New York except on Sundays, when the warrant for him could not be executed. When he was then held in criminal contempt, he sought refuge in Bimini, in the Bahamas. Shortly afterward, the House voted on March 1, 1967, to exclude Dr. Powell from the 90th Congress. His Harlem district promptly elected him, by 27,900 votes to 4,518, to fill the vacancy that his expulsion had created, and in 1969 the Supreme Court ruled that the House lacked authority to deny him his seat. Dr. Powell was hospitalized for treatment of cancer in 1969 and in the same year the Democratic Party denied him renomination for Congress. He died in Miami on April 4, 1972, and the boulevard, formerly the Harlem portion of Seventh Avenue, was named for him shortly afterward.

Dr. Adam Clayton Powell Jr. on Bimini in the Bahamas in 1960s.

Admiral George Dewey Promenade

The Namesake: the naval officer whose vastly superior fleet destroyed a Spanish flotilla in Manila Bay in 1898 without loss of a single American life. Dewey, who had served under Admiral David Farragut in the Civil War, was still on active duty at his death a few months before the U.S. entered World War I.

Two million New Yorkers gave Dewey a hero's welcome on September 30, 1899, with a parade down Broadway to 59th Street and down Fifth Avenue to Washington Square. But the cheers turned into jeers when Dewey, who was then 62, married a widow much younger than himself — and a Roman Catholic to boot — and compounded his crime by deeding to her a house in Washington, D.C., that Congress had bestowed on him. A temporary memorial arch on Madison Square, which was to have been replaced by one of marble, was carted off to a dump by the street cleaning department and the permanent memorial was never built. In 1965 the city made belated amends by naming the promenade by the harbor for Dewey.

Admiral Dewey on deck of the Olympia.

Albany Street

The Namesake: the first pier on the Hudson River side of Manhattan, built in 1797 to serve boats in the New York-Albany run. (They previously had used the more sheltered East River. The street led to the pier.)

Tiny Albany Street was the center of a controversy that raged for more than forty years, into the 1850s. The row concerned extension of Albany Street to Broadway through Trinity Churchyard. Trinity opposed the scheme and its proponents pictured the church as an "oppressor standing in the way of progress." William Curtis Noyes, addressing the Board of Aldermen in 1854 for more than thirty printed pages, orated: "What is the first requisite in a city of this description? Well ventilated, wide and accessible streets, so that a population like our own, active and industrious, may secure their health, comfort and convenience." Trinity objected that the churchyard contained the sacred bones of Revolutionary soldiers which should not be disturbed. "What Revolutionary soldiers?" the other side demanded, pointing out that the British had held the city throughout the Revolutionary War. Four times the extension of Albany Street won municipal approval. But somehow the extension was never carried out.

Sail and steam ships going up and down the North (Hudson) River, published in Gleason's Pictorial Drawing-Room Companion, March 26, 1853.

Adrian Avenue

The Namesake: Adriaen van der Donck, who in 1646 was granted a tract that extended from Spuyten Duyvil to Yonkers. He founded the City of Yonkers.

Van der Donck became New Amsterdam's first lawyer in 1653 but he was permitted only to advise clients, not to represent them in court. The reasoning was that since he was the only lawyer, his clients would have had an unfair advantage over their opponents. Both Adrian Avenue and Leyden Street, which was named for Leyden University in the Netherlands where Van der Donck got his law degree are in the Spuyten Duyvil area where Van der Donck had his land.

Alexander Hamilton Square

The Namesake: Alexander Hamilton, the Revolutionary War officer and first Secretary of the Treasury, who died in a duel with Aaron Burr.

Hamilton's home, The Grange, is situated there. Hamilton Place and Hamilton Terrace also are named for their proximity to the house.

Allen Street

The Namesake: Captain William Henry Allen, youngest skipper in the Navy in the War of 1812, and one of the most gallant. He died in action at the age of 29.

A midshipman at 16, Allen first served in the War of 1812 as a lieutenant to Stephen Decatur. New York gave him a hero's welcome on New Year's Day, 1813, when he brought the British ship *Macedonian* into the harbor as a prize. Promoted to command the brig *Argus*, Allen transported William H. Crawford to France to serve as American minister there, then roamed the English Channel for enemy craft. He captured twenty in a month, the last, unfortunately, a wine ship. When the British brig *Pelican* caught up with *Argus* on August 14, 1813, Allen's crew had a monumental, mass hangover. The first ball fired by *Pelican* carried away one of Allen's legs, but he refused to go below. He died the next day.

Capture (left, below) of the British ship Macedonian by Decatur and Allen in the War of 1812. "Captured after a spirited action of one hour & a half; sent in & arrived at New York."

Amsterdam Avenue

The Namesake: Amsterdam in the Netherlands, which sent the city's first settlers.

Amsterdam Avenue was part of Tenth Avenue until 1890, when residents above 59th Street argued that their neighborhood would benefit by a change of name. The Board of Aldermen decided at first to call it Holland Avenue, but switched to Amsterdam just before they passed their resolution. The board noted that other name changes, such as that of Eleventh Avenue to West End Avenue, had "had a marked and beneficial effect on property" and added that "in the several petitions the signers regard the proposed change of name as second in importance only to the advantages of increased rapid transit."

Ann Street

The Namesake: Ann White, wife of an early merchant and developer.

The land through which the street runs had been a governor's garden but as the city grew, the land became too valuable for a mere beauty spot: Captain Thomas White acquired it and cut it up into building lots. He named the street for his wife Ann, probably at her demand, because other land speculators already had named streets for their wives or daughters.

A. Philip Randolph Square

The Namesake: the founder and first president of the Brotherhood of Sleeping Car Porters, vice president of the AFL-CIO and long the country's best known black labor leader.

Asa Philip Randolph, who was born in Crescent City, Florida, in 1889, attended New York's City College and later received an LLD from Howard University. He organized the Pullman porters in 1925, a considerable feat at a time when the Pullman Company was anti-union, as was much of the nation, and most of the labor movement itself was racist. Randolph for decades fought discrimination in hiring, and his threat in World War II to lead a march on Washington impelled President Roosevelt to set up a Commission on Fair Employment Practices. After more than forty years at the head of the Brotherhood, Randolph became its president emeritus in 1968. The Brotherhood, its membership reduced by the decline in rail travel, merged in 1978 with the Brotherhood of Railway and Airline Clerks. The merged union's president, Fred J. Kroll, said at the time that the porters' organization, "in addition to performing its trade union functions, has served as a training school for many generations of responsible leaders of the black community in our country."

Arden Street

The Namesake: Jacob Arden, a butcher and Revolutionary patriot who owned property on Washington Heights between 170th and 176th streets.

Arden participated as a representative of his trade in a pre-Revolutionary demonstration against British rule, and in the war served as a private in a New York outfit. He died between 1778 and 1781, probably while fighting in the Ramapo Mountains area of Rockland County. His wife was one of the long line of women named Catherine Beekman in the long-established Beekman family (*see* Beekman Street).

Asser Levy Place

The Namesake: one of the earliest Jewish settlers, in 1654, and the city's first kosher butcher. (He had a gentile partner to handle the pork side of the business.) Levy bested Governor Peter Stuyvesant in a battle over religious discrimination — Stuyvesant tried to bar Levy and a fellow Jew from serving in the militia organized to defend the city. The Dutch West India Company directors in Amsterdam upheld Levy and he later became a leading citizen with an enviable reputation that extended far beyond the city's borders.

The street was named for him in 1954, the tercentenary of his arrival.

Astor Place

The Namesake: John Jacob Astor, originally Ashdor, who was the richest man in America when he died in 1848, age 75. The Astor family lived there.

Astor left Waldorf, near Heidelberg, Germany, when he was 16 to work in London for an uncle who was a partner in a piano factory. Four years later, in 1783, he sailed for Baltimore with a consignment of musical instruments and, aboard ship, heard about the fur trade. In New York, where his brother Heinrich was prospering as a butcher — Heinrich had accompanied British troops to this country — John Jacob got a job with a Quaker furrier. Later he set up shop on his own in Water Street, supplying furs to four London fur houses. He then went into shipping and real estate and amassed $30 million. The Waldorf-Astoria Hotel commemorates his name and that of his home town.

Attorney Street

The Namesake: presumably the lawyer or lawyers who had offices there.

The street was laid out before 1797, but when and for whom it was named have not been determined.

Audubon Avenue

The Namesake: John James Audubon, the half-French, half-Haitian naturalist and artist who painted North America's birds.

Audubon spent the last 11 years of his life in New York, most of them on a farm that extended from the Hudson to Amsterdam Avenue at what is now 155th Street. He died there in 1851.

The naturalist John James Audubon, painted 1826 by John Symmes.

Avenues A, B, C and D

Named in deference to practicality, manifested when the grid plan for the city's streets was adopted in 1811.

The alphabetically named avenues lie in an eastward bulge of Manhattan. Had they been designated numerically, First, Second, Third and Fourth avenues would have been truncated at, or just north of, Fourteenth Street, frustrating the planners' intent. The later opening of Madison, Lexington and Park avenues and the renaming of part of Fourth Avenue as Park Avenue South modified the scheme anyway.

Avenue of the Americas

The Namesakes: the members of the Organization of American States.

Formerly Sixth Avenue, the street was renamed as a flattering gesture to the nation's neighbors in the western hemisphere. But the gesture has remained just that—except on corporate letterheads and street signs, it's still Sixth Avenue to most New Yorkers.

Peace march up Avenue of the Americas, April 1968.

Avenue of the Finest

The Namesake: the New York Police Department.

The street was named in 1973 in connection with the opening of the new Police Headquarters at 1 Police Plaza, near City Hall.

Bache Plaza

The Namesake: Bache Halsey Stuart Shields, Inc., brokers and investment bankers whose headquarters are at 100 Gold Street, abutting Bache Plaza.

The firm is the result of the merger in the 1970s of several important brokerage houses, the largest of which, J.S. Bache & Company, was long headed by Jules S. (for Semon) Bache, owner of one of the world's finest private art collections. Born in New York in 1861 to a family of German-Jewish immigrants that had prospered richly here, Bache joined his uncle's brokerage house, Leopold Cahn & Company, as a cashier at the age of 19 in 1880; by 1892, he headed the house. Changing its name to J.S. Bache & Company, he rapidly established branches in this country and abroad and set it on the road to becoming America's second largest brokerage firm. Bache began collecting art in 1919, with the acquisition of Rembrandt's *Young Man in a Red Cloak*, and by 1929 had a store of Old Masters valued at many millions. After his death in Florida in 1944, at the age of 83, his collection went to the Metropolitan Museum of Art.

Bank Street

The Namesake: a branch of the Bank of New York, which had its main office on Wall Street.

A clerk in the bank's Wall Street headquarters was stricken with yellow fever in 1798, and, to avoid being quarantined and closed in the future, the bank bought eight lots on a nameless Greenwich Village lane and erected a branch there for use in emergencies. Bank Street boomed when an 1822 epidemic drove hundreds of city residents and businesses to the Village's more salubrious climate.

The Wall Street and subsequent Bank Street branches of the Bank of New York which moved "uptown" to avoid a plague of yellow fever in 1798.

Barclay Street

The Namesake: the Reverend Henry Barclay, who became the second rector of Trinity Church in 1746.

As a major landowner by royal grant and the church of many leading citizens, Trinity wielded great influence in city affairs and many street names derive from links to the church. But Barclay might have had a street named for him in any case. An Albany-born Harvard graduate, Barclay spoke the language of the Mohawk Indians as well as he did English and Dutch, and translated the liturgy into Mohawk. A panel in the bronze doors on the south side of the base of Trinity's tower depicts him preaching to the Indians in 1739, as his father had before him. In church he delivered sermons in English or Dutch as the occasion demanded, assuring himself wide regard. He married a daughter of Anthony Rutgers (see Rutgers Street).

Panoramic view from Broadway in 1854, looking west to Barclay Street (left) and Park Place (right), published in Gleason's Pictorial Drawing-Room Companion.

Barrow Street

The Namesake: Thomas Barrow, an artist who in 1807 drew a picture of Trinity Church that got wide circulation as a print.

Barrow Street was given its name at the request of Trinity Church. Originally, it was known as Reason Street, in honor of Tom Paine's *The Age of Reason*, but Reason had been corrupted into Raisin, so the rebaptism was in order.

Baruch Place and Baruch Drive

The Namesake: Dr. Simon Baruch, a German-Jewish immigrant who, while in his early twenties, served as a surgeon in General Robert E. Lee's army from 1862 to 1865 and then practiced medicine in Camden, South Carolina, until he moved to New York in 1881. As a famous physician on the Lower East Side, he crusaded for sanitation and introduced municipal bathhouses for the benefit of tenement dwellers. He was the father of Bernard Baruch, the financier and adviser to presidents. Dr. Baruch was 81 years old when he died in 1921.

The two streets' names were bestowed in 1933. Baruch Place formerly was Goerck Street, in honor of Casimir T. Goerck, a surveyor who prepared an 1803 map of the city.

Battery Place

The Namesake: a battery of artillery installed on a platform there in 1693 to protect the city against a French attack that never came.

The site remained a supposed military strongpoint during the War of 1812, having been reinforced by construction in 1807 of the West Battery, which was renamed Castle Clinton in 1815 in honor of Mayor DeWitt Clinton. Battery Park, which Battery Place borders, served as a prison camp for captured Confederates in the Civil War.

A view of the Battery and the harbor of New York, protected by a frigate, in the 1700's.

Bayard Street

The Namesake: Nicholas Bayard, nephew of Peter Stuyvesant and mayor of New York in 1686.

Bayard was largely responsible for the controversial hanging of Jacob Leisler, a popularly chosen governor (*see* Jacob Street and Frankfort Street). Bayard himself was convicted as an accomplice of the pirate Captain Kidd, but the death of King William saved Bayard from being hanged himself. The street bears his name because it formed part of the southern boundary of his estate, which extended from Canal to Bleecker and from Broadway to the Bowery.

Baxter Street

The Namesake: Charles Baxter, who resigned from the state legislature to enlist in the War of 1848 and, as a lieutenant colonel of the New York Regiment, was killed in the Battle of Chapultepec.

Baxter was given a public funeral at City Hall and was buried in Brooklyn's Greenwood Cemetery, where everybody who was anybody was laid to rest. (Before construction of Central Park, Greenwood was a fashionable place for Sunday strolling and picnicking.) Baxter Street originally was Orange Street, but Orange Street had become disreputable and the city fathers thought renaming it for a hero might elevate its morals.

Baxter (formerly Orange) Street at the notorious intersection called the Five Points, 1859.

Beach Street

The Namesake: Paul Bache, son-in-law of Anthony Lispenard, who owned the Lispenard Meadows just south of what is now Canal Street.

Beach is a corruption of Bache. Beach was the first street laid out on or adjacent to the Lispenard farm at the end of the 18th century.

Anthony Lispenard's meadows, engraved from a drawing by A. Anderson, 1785.

Beak Street

The Namesake: undetermined, but probably for a family living there when the street was named.

A new street (and tiny), Beak Street was named by the Board of Aldermen on May 11, 1925.

Beaver Street

The Namesake: the animal that contributed—involuntarily—to the city's fur trade, of which the street was the center in the early days. Beaver pelts served as money and were as good as gold.

The first openly recognized synagogue in North America is said to have stood in 1695 on the south side of Beaver Street between Broadway and Broad Street, opposite New Street: it served twenty families.

Provincial seal of Nieuw Nederland, 1623-1664.

Bedford Street

The Namesake: the street in London.

Bedford Street was mapped before 1799. Why it was named for the London street is not recorded.

Beekman Place

The Namesakes: the Beekman family, whose mansion, *Mount Pleasant*, was built by James Beekman in 1765 near the East River at what is now 51st Street. James Beekman was a descendant of Willem Beeckman, for whom Beekman Street was named.

The British made their headquarters in the mansion for a time during the Revolutionary War and Nathan Hale was tried as a spy in the mansion's greenhouse and hanged in the nearby orchard. George Washington visited the house often during his presidency. The Beekman family lived at *Mount Pleasant* until a cholera epidemic routed them in 1854 but the house survived until 1874, when it was torn down. With the surge of immigration from Europe in the late 19th and early 20th century, the Lower East Side's slums expanded north; the Beekman Place area's well-off residents gave way to impoverished workers in the *abattoire* and coalyards that defaced the East River shore. The neighborhood's rehabilitation began in the 1920s, powered in large part by Anne Morgan (of the Morgan banking family) and friends (*see* Sutton Place).

The Beekman mansion, "Mount Pleasant," used as headquarters by the British General Howe in the Revolutionary War.

Beekman Street

The Namesake: Willem Beeckman, who arrived in New Amsterdam from Holland in 1647 as a fellow passenger of Peter Stuyvesant. Beeckman got his start as a Dutch West India Company clerk and later served nine terms as mayor. He died in 1707, at the age of 85, leaving three sons and a daughter, the wife of Stuyvesant's son Nicholas William.

The street traverses the site of Beeckman's land, which extended from Nassau Street to the East River. Beeckman and his wife Catherine, whom he married here, first lived at Corlaer's Hook, which Beeckman bought from Jacobus van Corlaer. In 1670 Beeckman acquired Thomas Hall's farm and brewery in the vicinity of what is now Beekman Street. The farm included swampy ground useless for agriculture but good for tanning, and the area, soon known as Beekman's Swamp, became a leather goods center.

Bethune Street
The Namesake: Johanna Graham Bethune, early 19th-century philanthropist and educator who ceded the land for the street to the city.

Born at Fort Niagara, where her British father was a doctor, Johanna Graham was sent to school in Glasgow: a playmate there was the Walter Scott who became the novelist. Back in New York, she opened the city's first school for "young ladies," married the Reverend Divie Bethune, member of a wealthy and charitable family, and in 1806 joined Mrs. Alexander Hamilton in founding the New York Orphan Asylum at Barrow and Fourth streets.

Johanna Graham Bethune, educator and philanthropist.

Bennett Avenue
The Namesake: James Gordon Bennett the elder, founder of the *New York Herald*, which became part of the *New York Herald-Tribune,* the now defunct competitor of *The New York Times.* Bennett owned a country place in the vicinity of what is now Bennett Avenue.

A Scottish immigrant who had been educated for the Roman Catholic priesthood, Bennett started the *New York Herald* as a penny paper in a cellar in 1835. Initially, he served not only as editor and publisher but as the paper's newsboy. With *The Herald*, he introduced modern journalism to America. He was the first editor to report Wall Street financial news, the first to obtain the full texts of major speeches by telegraph, and among the earliest to use illustrations. During the Civil War, he had a large staff covering the battlefronts. At his death in 1872, his son and namesake took over the paper and it was the son who assigned Henry M. Stanley to find the missionary-explorer David Livingstone in the African wild.

The New York Herald, April 15, 1865, in its heyday under James Gordon Bennett.

Benson Street
The Namesake: Egbert Benson, New York's first attorney general. Appointed in 1777, he served for twelve years.

Benson was a member of the pre-Revolutionary Committee of Safety and later a delegate to the Continental Congress. He became a New York Supreme Court justice and a federal judge. He was a founder of the New-York Historical Society.

Logotype of the monthly newsletter of the New - York Historical Society.

Bloomfield Street
The Namesake: Brigadier General Joseph Bloomfield, a veteran of the Revolutionary War, who commanded New York's harbor defenses in the War of 1812.

The town of Bloomfield, New Jersey, was named for him in 1796. Bloomfield served as governor of New Jersey from 1801 to 1812, and in Congress from 1817 to 1821.

Bogardus Place

The Namesakes: the Bogardus family, who owned a large estate in the area of what is now Fort Tryon Park.

The first of the Bogarduses in America was the Reverend Everardus Bogardus, who arrived in 1633 and became the city's second clergyman. Prominent bearers of the name include James Bogardus, who in the 1840s pioneered in the construction of cast-iron buildings, some of which survive as landmarks. A new street, Bogardus Place was named in 1912.

James Bogardus, the architect.

Bowery

The Namesake: Peter Stuyvesant's farm, or *bouwerij,* to which the road led from the more settled parts of New Amsterdam. The farm's main house stood between 15th and 16th streets, just east of First Avenue.

George Washington gulped a quick one at the Bowery's Bull's Head Tavern before riding down to the waterfront to witness the departure of British troops in 1783. Not necessarily for that reason, the Bowery became, by the end of the 18th century, New York's most elegant street, lined with the mansions of prosperous residents and with fashionable shops. Lorenzo Da Ponte, the librettist for Mozart's *Don Giovanni, Marriage of Figaro* and *Cosi Fan Tutte,* ran one of the shops—a fruit and vegetable store—after he immigrated here in 1806. But by the time of the Civil War, the mansions and shops had given way to whorehouses, gigantic beer gardens and two-bit flophouses like the one at No. 15 in which the composer Stephen Foster lived in 1864.

The Bowery at its junction with Broadway, 1831, showing laborers, leveling the uneven terrain of Manhattan.

Bleecker Street

The Namesake: Anthony Bleecker, an early 19th-century Greenwich Village literatus.

The street, the land for which was deeded to the city in 1807, already ran through the Bleecker family farm. Anthony Bleecker was a friend of Washington Irving and William Cullen Bryant. His prose and poetry appeared in a variety of periodicals during some thirty years, and Bryant once reported that Eliza Fenno had left town in 1811 simply to get away from Bleecker's puns.

Once a Bleecker Street landmark, the mansion of Sir Peter Warren (see Warren Street) was built about 1745 and survived until 1865. Charlotte Warren, Lady Abingdon (see Abingdon Square) was born and grew up in the house.

Bond Street

The Namesake: undetermined. Named because of a suggestion by Samuel Jones, for whom Great Jones Street was named—at his own insistence (see Great Jones Street).

What prompted Jones to propose Bond Street's name may have been whimsy, since the northeast corner of Bond Street and Broadway in the early 1800s was the site of the mansion of Samuel Ward, a prominent banker. The mansion, which contained a splendid private library and art gallery, was eventually replaced by an early Brooks Brothers clothing store.

Bradhurst Avenue

The Namesake: Dr. Samuel Bradhurst, a physician who had an office and apothecary shop in Peck Slip in Revolutionary days, before the phrase "conflict of interest" was first spoken.

Dr. Bradhurst's two professions— doctor and druggist—enabled him to buy a country mansion neighboring Alexander Hamilton's The Grange. The doctor acquired the place about the end of the 18th century.

Peter Minuit buying Manhattan from the Indians, on the site that became Bowling Green.

Bowling Green

The Namesake: a field fenced off by the British in 1732 and leased to Frederick Philipse, John Chambers, and John Roosevelt for use as a private bowling area. The lease was for ten years and the rent was one peppercorn a year.

The green, where Peter Minuit closed his real estate deal with the Indians, lay in front of the city's first fort. Once part of the first livestock market (see Marketfield Street), it had also been used as a parade ground for the Dutch militia.

Pepper Plant.

Broadway

Named so because of its width, much greater in lower Manhattan in the city's early days than it is now.

Supposedly an Indian trail before the white man came, Broadway was called *Heere Straat* by the Dutch and Great George street by the British. Until its entire 15½-mile length was given a single name by law on February 14, 1899, Broadway from 59th Street to 155th Street was The Boulevard; from 155th to 157th streets the Boulevard Lafayette; from 157th Street to 170th Street it was Eleventh Avenue or The Boulevard again and from 170th Street to Spuyten Duyvil it was Kingsbridge Road.

Broadway between Howard and Grand Streets, 1840.

Bridge Street

The Namesake: a bridge that crossed Broad Street when that thoroughfare was an East River inlet known as the Broad Canal, or *de Heere Graft*.

The bridge was built for the convenience of residents of the houses that had risen on the sides of the canal. A mailbox nearby was specifically for trans-Atlantic mail. English and Dutch shopkeepers began in 1670 to gather there every Friday noon, giving rise to the first Merchants' Exchange.

The bridge crossing the Broad Canal, 1670.

Broadway Alley

The Namesake: undetermined.

The alley is off East 26th Street, near Third Avenue, several blocks from Broadway.

Broadway Terrace

The Namesake: Broadway, which Broadway Terrace abuts in the vicinity of West 193rd Street.

Broadway Terrace was named by the Board of Aldermen in 1911, at the time the terrace was created.

Broad Street

The Namesake: the Broad Canal, which the street replaced.

Originally an inlet of the East River, the canal was flanked by solid three-story houses, the paths in front of which were paved in 1660. The canal was filled in 1676 because fruit and vegetable vendors, including Indians who came by boat from Long Island, left the area littered.

Broome Street

The Namesake: John Broome, the first alderman chosen after the British evacuated New York in 1783, and Lieutenant Governor of the state in 1804.

A merchant who lived over his store in Hanover Square, Broome brought in two million pounds of tea from China at the end of the Revolutionary War and initiated the China trade on which hundreds of Americans grew rich.

Packet ships unloading imports at South Street and Maiden Lane, around 1828.

Bryant Park

The Namesake: William Cullen Bryant, journalist and poet.

Bryant, a New Englander of Pilgrim stock, came to New York in 1825 when he was 31, after nine years of practicing law, which he loathed. He was already renowned as a poet, having published *Thanatopsis*—written when he was not yet 18—in 1817. By 1829, he was editor and principal owner of the *New York Evening Post*, the newspaper founded by Alexander Hamilton. The paper survives as the tabloid *New York Post*. Bryant died in 1878, in his favorite month of June. The park and the adjoining New York Public Library at Fifth Avenue and Forty-secondStreet, which dates to 1904, occupy the site of the city's first great reservoir, inaugurated in the 1840s.

Cabrini Boulevard

The Namesake: Francesca Maria Cabrini, founder of the Missionary Sisters of the Sacred Heart and the first American citizen to become a Roman Catholic saint.

Mother Cabrini, who was born in Lombardy in 1850, was canonized as Saint Francesca Xavier Cabrini on July 7, 1946. But New York had anticipated the Church and had named the thoroughfare for her in 1938.

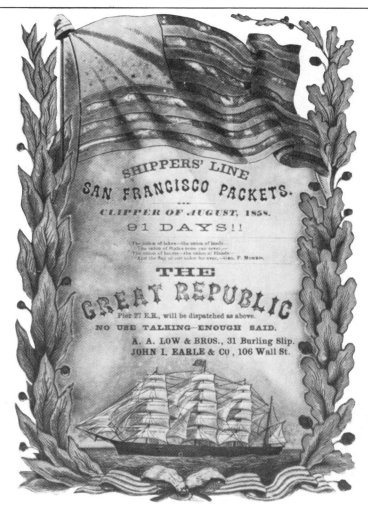

Burling Slip

The Namesakes: the Burling family, beginning with a pre-Revolutionary merchant and including William S. and Samuel Burling, late 18th-century and early 19th-century businessmen who had a glass and cabinet warehouse at 25-62 Beekman Street and used the slip for shipping.

Burling Slip existed by June 1752, when "at Burling's Slip, the new market" was advertised in the press. The market was not a success: on July 4, 1760, some 60 citizens petitioned for its abolition as a "common nusance to the publick" because "Idle people, Boys and Negroes" wasted time there "play-ing and Gaming." The market was closed in 1766. Burling's Slip was part of the ground on which the Battle of Golden Hill (*see* Gold Street) was fought in 1770 and the site of breastworks erected in 1776 immediately after word arrived of the Declaration of Independence. The slip later was known as Rodman's, but its name reverted to Burling, presumably in honor of William and Samuel. A public-spirited citizen, Samuel Burling in 1809 planted trees along Broadway from Leonard Street north to about Eighth Street.

The Great Republic clipper ship accepted cargo through merchants on Burling Slip in August 1858.

Canal Street

The Namesake: a 40-foot-wide canal, flanked by trees and a promenade, which was dug in 1805 to drain the Collect, or Fresh Water Pond (on the site of Foley Square), into the Hudson River.

Environmentalists opposed the canal because the Collect provided good fishing and ice skating. But precursors of Robert Moses said the pond bred mosquitoes and had to go. The canal too bred mosquitoes, though (and land in the area was becoming valuable), so after a decade both the canal and the muddy remains of the pond were filled in. A bridge that crossed the canal at Broadway was simply buried and incorporated into the road.

The 40-foot-wide canal, dug in 1805 to drain the Collect.

Cardinal Hayes Place

The Namesake: Patrick Joseph Hayes, a native New Yorker and an 1888 graduate of Manhattan College, who became Archbishop of New York in 1919 and a cardinal in 1924.

Cardinal Hayes died in 1938; the street was named for him in 1941.

Carlisle Street

The Namesake: Carlisle Pollock, one of three well-to-do Irish-born brothers who for many years in the late 18th century operated linen-importing businesses here and were active in the Society of the Friendly Sons of St. Patrick.

Carlisle Pollock was the father of St. Clair Pollock, the child buried in the lone grave in Riverside Park near Grant's Tomb. (see St. Clair Place). Carlisle Pollock owned a tract on the park site before 1800, but the 1797 City Directory gives his address as 11 Whitehall Street, his brother Hugh's as 3 Gouverneur's Alley and his brother George's as 91 Water Street.

Carmine Street

The Namesake: Nicholas Carman, an early vestryman of Trinity Church.

Originally Carman, the street's name somehow became Carmine. Edgar Allan Poe and his child bride Virginia once lived in a boardinghouse there.

Carl Schurz Park

The Namesake: Carl Schurz, hero of the German revolutionary movement of 1848-49, American diplomat, Union general, U.S. Senator, Secretary of the Interior, New York newspaper editor and civic reformer.

A tall, lanky fellow of unfailing humor and considerable talent as a pianist, Schurz as a youth wanted only a relaxed career as a professor of history in his native Germany. But he was fated to make history rather than teach it. As a 20-year-old student who had, to his surprise, proved to be a compelling orator, Schurz found himself a lieutenant and staff officer of the democratic forces in the abortive 1848-49 German rebellion. With the surrender of the fortress of Rastatt, which he had been sent to defend, he faced execution. He hid in the captured fort for four days, escaped through a sewer and made his way to Switzerland. At the same time a beloved professor of his had been arrested and sentenced to life imprisonment in Spandau. Schurz, armed with false passports, twice ventured back into Germany to rescue him. The job took nine months, but in the dark of a November night, the professor was lowered from one of the prison's attic windows. Schurz, with a carriage waiting, then whisked him to the coast and a tiny vessel that took them both to England. After

marrying in England, Schurz came to America in 1852 and in 1856 settled on a Wisconsin farm. He had not been there a year when his neighbors elected him a delegate to the state convention of the Republican party, which promptly nominated him for lieutenant governor though he was not yet a citizen. (He lost, so the issue of his eligibility did not come up.) Soon he was campaigning in Illinois for Abraham Lincoln against Stephen A. Douglas and in demand as a speaker in other states' elections. He headed Wisconsin's delegation to the 1860 National Republican Convention, which nominated Lincoln for the Presidency. After the campaign Lincoln wrote to him that "to the extent of our limited acquaintance, no man stands nearer my heart than yourself." Schurz was recruiting a regiment for the Union army when Lincoln appointed him Minister to Spain. But he resigned before a year had passed after failing to persuade the Lincoln administration to issue an immediate Emancipation Proclamation. He was then made a brigadier general, commanding a division, and soon was being mentioned in dispatches for his ability and personal courage. At the war's end, Schurz produced an extraordinarily valuable report in which he recommended that the southern states be required to

permit blacks to vote as a condition for readmittance to the Union. Schurz was editing a St. Louis newspaper when he was named temporary chairman and keynote speaker of the 1868 Republican convention that was to nominate General Ulysses S. Grant for the Presidency. Shortly thereafter, Schurz himself was elected, at age 39, U.S. Senator from Missouri. He had been in office only a few months when he introduced a bill, far ahead of its time, to establish a federal civil service based on merit. When a split in the Republican party cost him re-election to the Senate, President Rutherford B. Hayes, taking office March 4, 1877, named him Secretary of the Interior. Schurz's policies included enlightened treatment for Indians, development of national parks, protection of public lands and a departmental merit promotion system. When he left the cabinet in 1881, he moved to New York to become an editor of the *New York Evening Post* and *The Nation*. He spent the rest of his life here, opposing the war with Spain in 1898 and the subsequent annexation of the Philippines, serving as president of the National Civil Service Reform League and of the Civil Service Reform Association of New York.

Carl Schurz, photographed by Brady.

below: Carl Schurz speaking at the Fifth Avenue Hotel. 1876.

Cathedral Parkway

The Namesake: the Cathedral of St. John the Divine.

Cathedral Parkway was created by the widening of 110th Street between Seventh Avenue and Riverside Park. The work was authorized in April 1891; the cornerstone of the cathedral was laid Dec 27, 1892.

The Cathedral of St. John the Divine under construction, 1904.

Cedar Street

Like Pine and Cherry Streets, named after a tree—a relic of the forest that once covered Manhattan.

Originally, it was Little Queen Street, which had been laid out in 1692. It was renamed in 1794 in a belated flareup of anti-royalist sentiment that erased most reminders of the British era. The numerous changes of names made at that time encountered considerable opposition.

Central Park South

Named for its location at the lower boundary of the park, which itself is at the geographical center of Manhattan.

Just plain 59th Street before construction of the park began in an unkempt wilderness in 1858, Central Park South long has flourished as one of the most elegant thoroughfares in town and, it is likely, as the most cosmopolitan: its hotels, of which the Plaza is the stateliest, attract visitors from all over the world.

Catherine Lane

The Namesake: Catherine Rutgers (*see* Catherine Street, below).

Catherine Slip

The Namesake: Catherine Street (*see* below) from which it extends.

In the early 1800s, just before the advent of the steamboat, ferries powered by horses ran from Catherine Slip to Brooklyn. One horse-boat carried 543 passengers, plus carriages and carriage horses.

Catherine Street

The Namesake: Catherine Rutgers. She was a De Peyster before her marriage in 1732 to Hendrick Rutgers, who named the street after her.

Hendrick Rutgers owned the farm through which the street was cut. Rutgers Street is named for a son, Henry (*see* Rutgers Street). Lord & Taylor's first shop opened for business in 1826 at No. 47 Catherine Street, in a small three-story house with dormer windows.

Central Park North

Named for its location.

The northern border of Central Park, the street was 110th Street on the 1811 grid plan; it lies just east of Cathedral Parkway, which also was once 110th Street.

Central Park West
Again named for its location.

From *Frank Leslie's Illustrated Newspaper*, September 7, 1889

Formerly part of Eighth Avenue, Central Park West was renamed belatedly some years after completion of Central Park; like Amsterdam and West End avenues, among others, the boulevard was rebaptized for greater status. It already was, at 72nd Street, the site of the Dakota, built in 1884 and for many years the city's most famous apartment house. (The Dakota, financed by Edward Clark of Singer Sewing Machine wealth, owes its designation to its location, so far from the heart of town in 1884 that wags likened the area to the Dakotas.) Smaller apartment houses and a scattering of hotels began to rise before the turn of the century, but only in the early 1930s did Central Park West assume its present look. Virtually unique among the city's major thoroughfares, it has remained little changed for almost half a century.

The Dakota apartment house on Central Park West, from the south.

Centre Street

Named because of its situation, midway between the Hudson and East rivers.

The street's name long was synonymous with Police Headquarters.

Police headquarters on Centre Street, 1911.

Centre Market Place

The Namesake: Centre Market, which was situated just west of the street.

Centre Market Place, formerly atop a high hill, was named in 1839.

Chambers Street

The Namesake: John Chambers, lawyer, corporation counsel, alderman and Supreme Court judge between 1727 and his death, about 1765.

Chambers and another lawyer, Joseph Murray, were commended by the Common Council and given the freedom of the city in 1728 after they had returned fees of £5 each, paid them for legal work on the Council's behalf.

Charles Street

The Namesake: Charles Christopher Amos, who came into ownership of a section of Admiral Sir Peter Warren's large 18th-century Greenwich Village estate.

When streets were laid out on Amos's land, they were named Charles, Christopher and Amos. But the Amos did not stick: it became West 10th Street.

Charles H. Revson Plaza

The Namesake: Charles Haskell Revson, founder and mastermind of Revlon, Inc., the cosmetics manufacturer.

Son of a Russian immigrant, Revson came to New York when he was 17 from New England, where he had been born in 1906, and got a job in the garment industry. He was still in his early twenties when a chemist friend, Charles Lachman, heated some material over a Bunsen burner and showed him the result—a colorful, creamy fingernail enamel unlike anything then on the market. Revson, a brother, and Lachman scraped together $300 and in 1932 established Revlon, Inc., the letter l in the name representing a bow to Lachman. When Revson died in 1975, the company had revenues that year of $750 million and net earnings of $62.6 million. A terror to his executive employees, whom he fired like machine gun bullets, and a frequent subject of gossip about his private life, Revson has been described as crude and ruthless, but also as brilliant, honest and generous. The Charles H. Revson Plaza, which is at Columbia University, was named in recognition of his benefactions.

Charlton Street

The Namesake: Dr. John Charlton, an English surgeon who arrived with the British troops in the Revolutionary War and stayed on after the army departed.

Dr. Charlton served as president of the New York Medical Society. The street was given his name in 1807.

Chatham Square
The Namesake: William Pitt, Earl of Chatham and Prime Minister of Britain before the Revolution. Pitt Street also is named for him, and what is now Park Row formerly was Chatham Street.

A great orator and a manic-depressive genius, Pitt supported American opposition to the Stamp Act and constantly besought generous treatment for the Colonies, although he did not favor granting them independence. When New York erased most British names from its streets after the Revolution, Pitt and Chatham were gratefully retained. Since World War II, however, Chatham Square has acquired a Chinese alias. It is known as Kim Lau Square, in honor of a U.S. Air Force pilot of Chinese ancestry.

William Pitt the Elder, first Earl of Chatham, known as the Great Commoner.

Chelsea Square
The Namesake: London's Royal Chelsea Hospital for old soldiers.

In a mood of irony, Captain Thomas Clarke, a veteran of the French and Indian wars, gave the name Chelsea to a $5,000 farm he bought at 22nd Street west of Ninth Avenue, where he planned to live in retirement. He died soon afterward, but in 1777, his widow built a mansion there which she called Chelsea House. The Clarkes' son-in-law, Bishop Benjamin Moore, for whom North Moore Street is named, inherited Chelsea House, and his son Clement Clarke Moore, author of *'Twas the Night Before Christmas,* lived there after him. London Terrace, a row of elegant town houses that were replaced by the apartment house complex of the same name, was built just across 23rd Street from Chelsea House.

Cherry Street
The Namesake: a seven-acre cherry orchard that yielded the best cherries in town. It was owned by Goovert Loockermans, a wealthy merchant who was the New Amsterdam representative of the Amsterdam trading firm of Gillis Verbrugge & Co. in the 1660s.

Loockermans' heirs sold the land in 1672 for $60. Richard Sackett acquired part of it and opened a beer garden and a bowling green which became known as Sackett's Orchard. In 1789, George Washington lived in Cherry Street, in a four-story mansion that belonged to Walter Franklin, a wealthy merchant. Washington had just become President of the United States and Cherry Street thus was the site of the nation's first Executive Mansion.

Cherokee Place
The Namesake: the Cherokee Club, formerly a powerful satrapy of Tammany Hall.

The newly created, block-long street was named in 1913: the club's four-story red brick headquarters was nearby, on 79th Street betwen First and Second avenues. The building is now an apartment house.

The old Cherokee Club on East 79th Street.

Chisum Place
The Namesake: undetermined.

A tiny street abutting Harlem Houses at West 141st Street and the Harlem River Drive, Chisum Place was named on April 4, 1961, but neither the law that bestowed the name nor newspapers of the time record who was being honored.

Chittenden Avenue
The Namesake: Lucius Chittenden, who owned land from 185th to 198th streets.

Chittenden's house stood in what is now Fort Tryon Park. The avenue was named in 1911.

Claremont Avenue

The Namesake: Claremont Mansion, built early in the 19th Century in what is now Riverside Park, on a site that George Washington had proposed for the U.S. Capitol. It became an inn before the Civil War.

Nicholas de Peyster sold the mansion's site to George Pollock in 1796; George Pollock's brother Carlisle (*see* Carlisle Street) had a neighboring estate. Michael Hogan, a millionaire Irish immigrant, acquired the place in 1804 from Joseph Alston, the husband of Aaron Burr's daughter, Theodosia. Hogan named his mansion Claremont for his native county Clare and for Claremont Castle, residence of his old buddy the Duke of Clarence who became King William IV. The Earl of Devon watched from Claremont in 1807, when Robert Fulton tested his steamship *Clermont* in the river.

Claremont Inn in 1932.

Christopher Street

The Namesake: Charles Christopher Amos (*see* Charles Street).

Christopher Street formerly was called Skinner Road in honor of Colonel William Skinner, a son-in-law of Admiral Sir Peter Warren, who owned most of the Village in the mid-1700s.

Church Street

The Namesake: Trinity Church.

The street existed as early as 1761 and was extended in 1784; the portion owned by Trinity Church was ceded to the city in 1804.

City Hall Park and Square

The Namesake: City Hall, which overlooks the park and square.

The park and square occupy the site of a free pasture known in Dutch days as *De Vlackte* (the Flat) and later as the Commons. The present City Hall, New York's third, was built at its northern end in 1803.

Chrystie Street

The Namesake: Lieutenant Colonel John Chrystie, an 1806 graduate of Columbia College, who died in the War of 1812.

Against great odds, Chrystie led two attacks across a river at the Battle of Queenstown Heights on October 13, 1812. Wounded and captured, he died of what was described as "bilious colic" on July 22, 1813.

The Battle of Queenstown Heights, October 13, 1812; two attacks across the river were led by Lt. Col. John Chrystie.

Clarkson Street

The Namesake: Matthew Clarkson, a youthful Revolutionary soldier who became a legislator, philanthropist and banker.

A volunteer in the Battle of Long Island, Clarkson later served as an aide to General Benedict Arnold and on the staff of General Ben Lincoln. After the war, he was an assemblyman (and introduced a bill to abolish slavery in New York), a state senator, a U.S. marshal and a member of the Board of Regents of the State University of New York. His numerous philanthropic activities included the presidency of New York Hospital, and his business life the presidency of the Bank of New York from 1804 to 1825, the year he died. He was known as General Clarkson because he held the rank of major-general in the New York State militia. The street named for him by the Common Council in 1807 was originally called Morton Street (see Morton Street).

Cleveland Place

The Namesake: Stephen Grover Cleveland, President of the United States (1885-89 and 1893-97).

An upstater, Cleveland had limited association with New York City but he once worked here: after his minister father's death, he spent a year, from the fall of 1853 to the fall of 1854, as an assistant teacher at the New York Institution for the Blind, whose building stood between 33rd and 34th streets and between Eighth and Ninth avenues. Cleveland later moved on to Buffalo, where he became a lawyer, mayor and then governor of New York State.

Cliff Street

The Namesake: Dirck van der Clyff, who owned the property on which the street was cut early in the 18th century.

Although the street had been laid out long before, it was not opened until 1786.

Clinton Street

The Namesake: George Clinton, Revolutionary War general and first governor of New York under the post-Independence state constitution.

George Clinton served as governor for 18 successive years, from 1777 to 1795, and three more years from 1801 to 1804. He became vice president of the United States in 1804 and retained the post until he died in 1812. He was the uncle of DeWitt Clinton, his secretary, who was elected to the U.S. Senate in 1802; he resigned to assume the mayoralty of New York City, and went on to become governor. Clinton Street was named in 1792; before that, it was called Warren Street.

General George Clinton, first Governor of New York State.

Coenties Slip and Alley

The Namesake: Conraet Ten Eyck and his wife Antje, who lived there in Dutch days. The name *Coenties* is a diminutive of "Conraet's and Antje's."

The first City Hall stood at Coenties Alley and Pearl Street, on a site that recently has been a parking lot (see Pearl Street). The slip, an artificial inlet in the East River for tying up ships, was filled in 1835.

The first City Hall at Coenties Alley and Pearl Street, 1679.

Columbus Avenue

The Namesake: Christopher Columbus.

Ninth Avenue above 59th Street was renamed for the explorer in 1890, two years before the 400th anniversary of his voyage to the Americas. But there was more behind the change than belated recognition for Columbus: above 59th Street, the avenue was residential and people who lived on it wanted it distinguished from the part occupied by trade.

Christopher Columbus.

Columbia Street
The Namesake: Columbus's New World.

Jersey Street and Grove Street both have borne the name Columbia, but the present Columbia Street, which extends south from Avenue D, appears to have the oldest, though not quite legitimate, claim to it. The street traverses the site of Peter Stuyvesant's farm and the name Columbia Street dates way back, but, curiously, has never been officially adopted.

Columbus Circle
The Namesake: Columbus' monument.

The circle was named in 1892 when the monument, sculpted by Gaetano Russo, was presented to the city by residents of Italian origin to mark the 400th anniversary of Columbus' voyage.

Columbus Circle, twenty years after the central monument was installed.

Collister Street
The Namesake: "Tommy" Collister, sexton of Trinity Church from 1790 to 1816, and assistant sexton for several years before that.

The street dates to 1818.

Commerce Street
Named for the business firms that moved in *en masse* when a smallpox epidemic paralyzed the city proper in 1822.

The street used to be called Cherry Lane, a name perpetuated by the Cherry Lane Theater.

Convent Avenue
The Namesake: the Convent of the Sacred Heart, which stood betwen 126th and 135th streets and between 10th and St. Nicholas avenues.

The convent burned down on August 13, 1888.

Cooper Square
The Namesake: Peter Cooper, the 19th-century industrialist, inventor and philanthropist.

Cooper once ran a grocery store across the street from the site of Cooper Union, which he founded. Though he had no schooling, Cooper designed and built America's first steam locomotive, the *Tom Thumb,* and the foundries he established greatly advanced the methods of producing iron. In 1876 he was the Greenback Party nominee for President.

Peter Cooper in 1876 at age 85, when he ran for the Presidency.

Cooper Street
The Namesake: James Fenimore Cooper, author of *"The Last of the Mohicans"* and more than two dozen other novels.

Cooper grew up and died in Cooperstown, New York, which his congressman-father founded. But during his writing career, he was a New York man-about-town, living on Broadway and dominating a literary society called the Bread and Cheese Club.

Corlear Place, formerly van Corlear Place
The Namesake: uncertain; probably was Arent van Curler or van Corlaer. (He signed himself van Curler.)

Arriving in New Netherland in 1638, age 18, Arent van Curler first worked for his great-uncle, Kiliaen van Rensselaer, patroon of Rensselaerswyck up the Hudson. Starting in a lowly job, he won steady promotions to the rank of commissary, in charge of the flow and distribution of supplies and when he was 24, he married Anthonia, the widow of Jonas Bronck, for whom The Bronx is named. (Corlear Place is close to the border between The Bronx and Manhattan.) Van Curler was beloved by the Indians and was on his way to Canada with several of them to meet Canadian dignitaries when he drowned in a sudden storm on Lake Champlain. The scene of the tragedy thereafter was known as Corlaer's Bay. The Indians bestowed another posthumous honor on him: after the British took over New Netherland, the Indians called each British governor by the title *Corlaer.*

Cornelia Street
The Namesake: the granddaughter of Robert Herring, on whose farm the street was laid out in 1794.

The Herring family—originally Harinck—were early Dutch settlers.

Cortlandt Street in the early 19th century.

Cortlandt Street

The Namesake: the Van Cortlandt family, of whom the first to settle here was Oloff Stevensen van Cortlandt; he arrived in 1637 as a Dutch soldier, amassed a fortune as a brewer and served as burgomaster from 1655 to 1665. He married the daughter of Goovert Loockermans (see Cherry Street).

Van Cortlandt's estate on the west side of Broadway was in the vicinity of what became Cortlandt Street.

Oloff Stevensen's sons Stephanus and Jacobus both were mayors under British rule and Stephanus introduced street cleaning to New York. The site of Van Cortlandt Park in the Bronx, where Mohican Indians used to hunt, came into the family's hands when Frederick Philipse gave it to his adopted daughter Eva, wife of Jacobus. The city bought it from Eva's and Jacobus's descendants in 1899.

Cortlandt Alley

See Cortlandt Street.

Crosby Street

The Namesake: William Bedlow Crosby, early 19th-century philanthropist.

When both of his parents died two years after his birth in 1786, Crosby was adopted by his mother's uncle, Henry Rutgers (see Rutgers Street). Crosby inherited the Rutgers wealth and devoted his life to good works.

William Bedlow Crosby (1786-1865) painted by Samuel Lovett Waldo.

Cumming Street

The Namesake: a property owner there early in this century.

Cumming Street was named May 11, 1925.

Cuylers Alley

The Namesake: Henry Cuyler, who owned the adjacent land when the street became a thoroughfare in 1803.

The first Cuyler settled in Albany in 1664. The family owned a sugar warehouse at Duane and Rose streets in Manhattan. Cuylers Alley already existed when the city mapped it and ordered it paved.

Delancey Street

The Namesake: James de Lancey, who became a New York Supreme Court judge in 1731, at the age of 28, and who served as Chief Justice from 1733 until he died in 1760. While on the bench he was New York's lieutenant governor from 1753 to 1755 and from 1757 to 1760. Though irreligious, he was for many years politically and personally the most influential man in the colony.

James de Lancey's father Étienne, a Protestant refugee from persecution by France's King Louis XIV, amassed a half-million-dollar fortune as a merchant after his arrival here with the family jewels; he married the former Anne van Cortlandt and built the big warehouse of which the remains are incorporated in Fraunces Tavern. Delancey Street marks the northern boundary of the De Lancey estate, which extended from the Bowery to the East River and from Stanton to Division streets. Encompassing 120 blocks, it was the largest estate then owned by a single family on Manhattan Island.

Fraunces Tavern in 1777, formerly a De Lancey residence and then a warehouse.

Depew Place

The Namesake: Chauncey Mitchell Depew, lawyer, legislator, railroad president and wit.

Appointed the first U.S. Minister to Japan in 1866, at the age of 32, Depew was induced by Cornelius Vanderbilt to turn down the job and became instead an attorney for Vanderbilt's railroad interests. Vanderbilt offered him less money than the $7500 that the diplomatic post paid, but promised him a greater future: Depew eventually became president of the New York Central. He served two terms in the U.S. Senate—1900 to 1912—after resigning the road's presidency. He died in 1928.

Chauncey Mitchell Depew, president of the New York Central Railroad.

Depeyster Street

The Namesake: Abraham de Peyster, mayor from 1691 to 1695 and later Chief Justice and acting governor.

The street follows the course of the driveway to the house of Johannes de Peyster, Abraham's father, who was asked to serve as mayor but declined on the ground that he did not speak English. Abraham donated the site for the city's second City Hall, which was built at Wall and Nassau streets in 1704, and remodelled in 1788 by Major Pierre Charles l'Enfant as Federal Hall; George Washington took his oath as President there. A statue of Abraham, executed in 1896, stands in Bowling Green. The family silver is exhibited at the New-York Historical Society.

Statue of Abraham de Peyster, sculpted by George Bissell in 1896; it stands in Hanover Square.

Desbrosses Street
The Namesake: Elias Desbrosses, pre-Revolutionary alderman and third president of the New York Chamber of Commerce.

A native New Yorker of Huguenot ancestry, Desbrosses started his career as a confectioner, but went into the export-import business, trading chiefly with the West Indies and Madeira. When he died in 1778, he was one of the city's biggest real estate owners.

Dey Street
The Namesake: Dirck Theunis Dey, who leased a royal farm in 1677.

Dey's farm extended from his house on a hill close to Broadway down to the Hudson River. The street follows a road cut through the farm when ferry service to New Jersey started in 1763. The ferry ran to Paulus Hook, now Jersey City.

Division Street
The Namesake: the dividing line between the farms of James de Lancey and Henry Rutgers. The space occupied by the street was a kind of no-man's-land used for a rope walk, i.e. a place where hemp was twisted into rope.

(See Delancey Street, Catherine Street, Henry Street and Rutgers Street).

Donnellon Square
The Namesake: a resident of the area killed serving in World War I. Nothing more is known about him.

The square was named by the Board of Aldermen on May 2, 1921.

Dominick Street
The Namesake: Georges Dominick, a mid-18th-century refugee from France who became a vestryman of Trinity Church and a captain in the militia.

Georges and his brother François, who were business partners, lived on Cherry Street.

Dongan Place
The Namesake: Colonel Thomas Dongan, first Roman Catholic governor of New York (1683—1688) and sponsor of the Charter of Liberties and Privileges (Dongan's Charter) which became New York's first genuine constitution. He succeeded to the title Earl of Limerick.

A liberal Irishman, Dongan won broad Protestant support in a time of religious tensions and courageously disobeyed royal orders that he considered unfair to colonists or Indians. Fired for good behavior, he retired to an estate on Staten Island, where Dongan Hills is named for him.

Seal on the Dongan charter.

Downing Street
The Namesake: doubtful

The street was laid out before 1799 and the name has been attributed to Downing's, an oyster house first established in the cellar of No. 5 Broad Street by a black restaurateur whose given name has been forgotten. Under the founder's son, George T. Downing, the place became a headquarters for politicos and businessmen in the 1830s: wine and vinegar from Downing's storerooms are said to have been poured on the flames in the great fire of 1835 that devastated New York. Another possible namesake is the Sir George Downing whom London's Downing Street commemorates. That Downing was one of the nine graduates of Harvard in the class of 1642—at the university's first commencement. (He stood second in rank.) Returning to his native England, he joined Oliver Cromwell's forces, did well for himself and became Cromwell's envoy to France and then to The Hague. After Cromwell's death, he tested the political winds and joined the Royalists, cozying up to Charles II, who knighted him and sent him back to The Hague as ambassador extraordinary. (In the course of his switch, he betrayed his old friend and colonel in Cromwell's forces and sent him to the executioner in London: Samuel Pepys, with whom he once worked, described Downing as "an arrant villain and ingrate." His possible claim to immortalization here—in the naming of Downing Street—is based on the fact that he was Britain's envoy in the Netherlands when the Dutch handed over New Orange (New Amsterdam) to the British in 1674 in exchange for Surinam. Although he was not the chief negotiator of the deal, historians suspect that he played an influential part.

Dover Street

The Namesake: the English Channel port.

On the East River, Dover Street (at Pearl) was the Manhattan base for the first ferry to Brooklyn, which began running in 1638. For British sailors whose men-o'-war docked there, the temptation to liken the river to the Channel and the docks to Dover's may have been overwhelming.

Doyers Street

The Namesake: Anthony H. Doyer, a distiller of Dutch origin who established a tea garden at the close of the 18th century on land that had been part of the Rutgers family farm. The garden was a popular meeting place for local gentry.

About 1809, Doyer built a house at No. 3 Doyers (a corruption of Doyer's) Street. When Chinese moved into the area in the mid-19th century, one Ah Quong occupied the cellar of No. 3; he spent night after night tapping the walls and digging up the basement floor in search of a $35-million fortune that Doyer, legend had it, had hidden. The story of the buried treasure—always the preposterous sum of $35 million—persisted for 75 years.

Duffy Square

The Namesake: Father Francis P. Duffy, whose statue stands in the square.

Father Duffy was chaplain of the 165th U.S. Infantry (the old 69th New York), in which he held the rank of lieutenant colonel. He served in the Spanish-American War, the Mexican border incident and World War I, in which he won the Distinguished Service Cross twice, the Distinguished Service Medal, the Legion d'Honneur and the Croix de Guerre. He died in 1932.

Duane Street

The Namesake: James Duane, first mayor of New York after the British evacuated the city in 1783. President Washington later made him a U.S. District Court judge.

An attorney, Duane defended Trinity Church in the interminable legal action brought by some of the heirs of Anneke Jans, who claimed to be the rightful owners of the downtown Manhattan land awarded to the church by the British Crown. Duane was a friend of Alexander Hamilton.

"Soda Fountain Rag," in 1915, when he was 16, before he could read music. He created it out of his experience as an after-school soda jerk; later, his bent for painting earned him a good living as a sign painter but by 1918 he had his own band. West 106th Street, where he owned a mansion, was renamed Duke Ellington Boulevard—West 106th Street on October 7, 1977. The street runs from Riverside Drive to Central Park West.

left: Poster advertising "Duke" Ellington and his Band.

below: "Duke" Ellington in 1929.

Duke Ellington Boulevard—West 106th Street

The Namesake: Duke (Edward Kennedy) Ellington, composer, bandleader and pianist whose 900 works ranged from popular classics such as "Mood Indigo" to sacred music and symphonies.

Born in Washington, D.C., where his father was a skilled worker in the Navy Department, Ellington acquired the nickname Duke in childhood because of the elegance of his dress and manner. He was largely self-taught as a musician and produced his first composition,

Dutch Street
The Namesakes: The city's founders.

The street was laid out before 1730 but it remained nameless until it was graded in 1789.

Dyckman Street
The Namesakes: The Dyckman family, which once owned much of upper Manhattan; at the time of the Civil War, their 400-acre farm was the largest on the island.

The first Dyckman, Jan, arrived from Westphalia in the mid-17th century: a bookkeeper, he worked prodigiously as a woodcutter and amassed enough money to start acquiring land in partnership with Jan Nagel (see Nagle Avenue). He married Nagel's widow. A bequest from his father-in-law also helped, and at his death he was a major real estate owner. Jan's great grandsons distinguished themselves in the Revolution as guides to the patriot forces. The still surviving Dyckman homestead at 204th Street and Broadway, the only Revolutionary era farmhouse remaining on Manhattan, was built by William Dyckman after British troops burned down its predecessor.

The Dyckman house on Broadway at 204th Street.

Dyer Avenue
The Namesake: George Rathbone Dyer, chairman of the board of the Port of New York Authority when he died, age 66, on August 31, 1934, a few months after having broken ground for the Lincoln Tunnel.

A financier in private life and a 44-year veteran of the National Guard, in which he rose from private to major-general, Dyer devoted 23 years of unpaid service, mostly as chairman, to the New York State Bridge and Tunnel Commission, which constructed the Holland Tunnel and the George Washington Bridge; when the commission was superseded by the Port Authority, he was appointed to the successor entity and later became its presiding officer. Upon his death, a letter to The New York Times suggested that what is now the Lincoln Tunnel be named the Dyer Tunnel; the procession of his military funeral took an hour and a half to march from 34th Street and Park Avenue to 90th Street and Fifth Avenue.
The avenue named for him was constructed to serve Lincoln Tunnel traffic.

East Broadway
The Namesake: Broadway, which it was expected to relieve of traffic jams.

East Broadway, which shoots northward from Chatham Square, was named about 1830. It began as a lane before 1732, when Herman Rutgers, who was a brewer, was buying up land east of the Bowery.

East End Avenue
The Namesake: its location.

Running from 79th Street to 90th Street, it is the easternmost street in the area.

East Houston Street
(See Houston Street.)

East Houston Street was formerly called North Street, because in the early 19th century it formed part of the city's northern boundary.

Edgar Street
The Namesakes: the Edgar family, to whose mansion on Greenwich Street the little road led. William Edgar's address is listed in a 1786 city directory as 7 Wall Street but the Edgars' shipping trade had warehouses on Broadway and by the 1830s their firm was the biggest of its kind in the city.

Sixty or so feet long, Edgar Street is the shortest in Manhattan. In Dutch days it was called Tuyn Paat, which means Garden Lane: the British corrupted that to Tin Pot Alley. Edgar Street now lies thirty feet north of its original location, having been shifted in 1953.

Edwin M. Morgan Place
The Namesake: a New York Postmaster appointed in 1897. He died in office in 1925.

A mailman before he was 16 years old, Morgan was described by his predecessor in the New York Postmastership as "the best post office man in the United States."

Eldridge Street
The Namesake: Lieuenant Joseph C. Eldridge, killed in ambush by Canadian Indians in the War of 1812.

Originally known as Third Street, Eldridge Street was laid out on James de Lancey's farm before 1767 and was renamed after Eldridge's death in 1813.

East River Drive, also called the
Franklin D. Roosevelt Drive
The Namesake: the river it parallels.

The first section of the drive, the
three and a half miles from Grand
Street to 60th Street, was initiated in
1936 by Borough President Samuel
Levy and Mayor Fiorello H. La
Guardia. It was designed as part of a
"comprehensive arterial highway
system" around Manhattan. The
drive was dedicated June 18, 1940.

Mayor La Guardia cutting the ribbon at the
opening of the East River Drive, 1940.

Edgecombe Avenue
The Namesake: its location at the
crest of a hill, for which the Saxon
word is *combe*.

The name was suggested by the
West Side Association in 1872.

Crowd watching a baseball game at the Polo
Grounds from Coogan's Bluff, Edgecombe
Avenue, around 1905.

Elizabeth Street
The Namesake: undetermined, but probably the wife or daughter of the landowner whose property the street ran through.

Elizabeth Street was laid out before 1755 in a shorter version than its present form: it was extended to Bleecker Street in 1816.

Elk Street
The Namesake: the Benevolent and Protective Order of Elks, New York Lodge #1.

The Jolly Corks, a drinking club of theatrical people which developed into the fraternal and philanthropic society, held its first formal session in the attic of Mrs. Giesman's boardinghouse on Elm Street, in 1867. When the club became a lodge, the members chose the elk as their symbol because it was handsome, fleet of foot, and peaceable unless attacked. Elm Street's name was changed to Elk in 1939 in the order's honor.

Photo of the Elk's symbol and guest, 1908

Ellwood Street
The Namesake: undetermined.

Like a number of other streets in northern Manhattan, Ellwood traverses the old Dyckman lands. The street was laid out in 1891 and named in 1911, but for whom nobody now knows. When the street was cut, workmen uncovered the remains of what obviously had been crude military shelters, presumably occupied during the Revolutionary War. The troops who lived in them are believed to have been Hessians: the belief is based on the fact that British forces dominated Manhattan for most of the war but no buttons from English uniforms were found among the relics.

Ericsson Place
The Namesake: John Ericsson, designer of *Monitor*, the first ironclad battleship.

Ericsson lived between 1864 and 1889 at 36 Beach Street; Ericsson Place is actually part of Beach Street.

Ericsson as depicted in Century Magazine.

Exterior Street
The Namesake: its situation on Manhattan's Harlem River shore.

The street was created to accommodate industry at the time the Harlem River Drive was built.

Exchange Place and Exchange Alley
The Namesake: the Merchants Exchange formally established in 1670 but in existence even earlier.

Once a pasture and then a garden, Exchange Place originally was called *Tuyn* or *Tuijn* Street. Later it became Garden Street, the English version of *Tuyn* or *Tuijn*. An imposing building that resembled the present City Hall was erected for the Exchange at Wall and William streets between 1825 and 1827. Destroyed in the Great Fire of 1835, the structure was replaced by an equally imposing one on the same site in 1842. The new Exchange became the Custom House in 1863; in this century, the National City Bank, now part of Citicorp, took it over and incorporated it into a taller office building.

The fire of 1835 (which destroyed the first Merchants' Exchange) as seen from Wall and William Streets.

Essex Street
The Namesake: the English county of that name.

Extra Place
The Namesake: what was left over after Philip Minthorne, who died in 1802, divided his 110-acre farm equally among his four sons and five daughters.

This tiny street is off East First, near Second Avenue. The original farm was a triangle with a long side on Broadway.

Fairview Avenue
The Namesake: its topography.

Although most of the avenue belies its name, the outlook northward from the avenue's northern end atop Fort George Hill is impressive.

Father Demo Square
The Namesake: Father Antonio Demo, Italian-born priest who served the Church of Our Lady of Pompeii in Carmine Street for 35 years.

Father Demo built the present church at Carmine and Bleecker streets in 1925. Mayor Fiorello LaGuardia named the square after Father Demo's death in 1936.

Ferris wheel set up in Father Demo Square for the 1975 Festa Italiana and the 50th anniversary of the Church of Our Lady of Pompeii. (at left)

Father Fagan Park
The Namesake: the Reverend Richard Fagan, a youthful Franciscan who was attached to the staff of the Church of St. Anthony of Padua at 153 Sullivan Street.

Father Fagan, who was 27, died in a fire on November 4, 1938, that swept the church's monastery at 151 Thompson Street. More than 1,000 people attended his funeral, at which it was said in the eulogy that he had died a hero, attempting to save others.

Fifth Avenue
The Namesake: its position in the city plan completed on March 22, 1811.

Fifth Avenue, whose mere number has become a world-renowned name, had an unpromising start: in 1811, it consisted of two parallel lines on a map. The territory through which it was designed to run—someday—remained a wilderness of hills and dales, punctuated by far-apart farms and an occasional hamlet. Creation of Washington Square (*see* Washington Square) gave the avenue its first impetus toward realization: construction of the avenue between Art Street (now Waverly Place) and 13th Street began in November 1824; an extension to 24th St. was added in 1830, and by 1864 the avenue stretched all the way to Harlem. But Charles Dickens, visiting New York in 1842, apparently did not notice the avenue, for he never mentioned it. When the Croton Reservoir (on the site of the New York Public Library at 42nd Street) filled up for the first time a few years later, the area was a pleasant place to go by carriage for a day in the country. And when the great marble Fifth Avenue Hotel opened at Madison Square in 1859, it was considered so far out that its proprietor offered elegant rooms with bath and four splendid meals a day for $2.50 to attract guests. The avenue entered its heyday about the time of the Civil War: *Leslie's Weekly* in December 1865 commented that "Fifth Avenue, at present . . . a street of 45 blocks . . . has upon it 340 residences, all of the finer class, except for a few shanties near the Park. It may safely be said that of these 340 houses, not one cost less than $20,000." Houses that cost vastly more soon followed. Astors and Vanderbilts, along with lesser millionaires, moved to the Avenue from downtown and mansions rose along it as far north as 57th Street. Feuding branches of the Astor family began the Waldorf Hotel in 1893 and the Astoria Hotel in 1897, then reluctantly united the two establishments as the Waldorf-Astoria. (The Empire State Building, built in 1933, occupies the great hotel's site.) Trade invaded the avenue when B. Altman's moved from Third Avenue and 10th Street to 34th Street, across from the Waldorf-Astoria.

Sunday on Fifth Avenue in 1898

Finn Square

The Namesake: Philip S. Finn, a member of the "Fighting 69th" Regiment, who was killed in France in World War I. The regiment, officially the 69th New York, was the one in which Father Duffy (*see* Duffy

Square) also served.

Philip Finn was a son of the Tammany leader, "Battery Dan" Finn.

The "Fighting 69th," returning home at the end of World War I.

Fletcher Street

The Namesake: Benjamin Fletcher, royal governor of New York from 1692 to 1698.

Fletcher gave New York its start as a printing center—albeit unintentionally—when he awarded the first governmental printing contracts to William Bradford, a Philadelphian who had moved here after a schism with fellow Quakers. Fletcher's interpretation of an act passed by the New York Assembly gave the Church of England status here as the established church of the colony. It was Fletcher who in 1693 installed the guns from which the Battery got its name.

Florence Place

The Namesake: undetermined.

Florence Place was authorized by the Board of Aldermen on July 1, 1913, for the enlargement of Market Street between Forsyth and Divison streets.

Forsyth Street

The Namesake: Lt. Col. Benjamin Forsyth, a North Carolinian hero of the War of 1812.

Forsyth was killed in action in upstate New York in June 1814 while fighting a much stronger force of British and Indians. Until 1817, Forsyth Street was called Second Street.

Fort Charles Place

The Namesake: Fort Prince Charles, which was named for Prince Charles Frederick, the brother-in-law of King George III.

The fort was built by American Revolutionary soldiers in 1776, but the British captured it in a minor battle in January 1777 and gave it its name.

Foley Square

The Namesake: Thomas F. (Big Tom) Foley, political godfather of Alfred E. Smith. When he died in 1925, *The New York Times* described him as "virtually the last of the old-time Tammany district leaders."

Wresting a Tammany district leadership from 'Paddy' Diver in 1901, Foley remained an unchallengeable power in lower Manhattan until his death. Born poor in Brooklyn's Williamsburg, Foley went to work at age 13 on the death of his father; he was a butcher's delivery boy and a blacksmith's helper before becoming a saloonkeeper in Williamsburg and then on the Lower East Side. But his true vocation was politics, in the pursuit of which he acquired a reputation for generosity, sagacity and a measure of humility. In the three stories above one saloon that he owned in South Street, he maintained more than a score of beds for derelicts, whom he fed free. Later in life he borrowed $137,500 from Charles Stoneham—the owner of the New

"Big Tom" Foley, photographed by George Grantham Bain.

York Giants baseball team—in a vain attempt to save the husband of an old neighbor from bankruptcy. Al Smith, who was associated with him for more than a quarter of a century, said of him after his death: "His days and nights were spent in the uplift of the poor and lowly, the afflicted and the unfortunate, the weak and the downtrodden." In a day when Tammany Hall and corruption were practically synonymous, even his daughter believed him to have become a millionaire, but he left an estate of a mere $15,000—he apparently had given away with one hand whatever he had taken in with the other. Foley served on the old City Council until it was abolished when Greater New York was established in 1898, then as an alderman, and in 1907 one term as sheriff. But he declined higher public office and the leadership of Tammany Hall on the ground that he was only a saloonkeeper. He was proudest of having chosen Al Smith for election to the New York State Assembly, from which Smith went on to become governor. Foley Square, the site of his last saloon—which was a meeting place for lawyers and politicians—was named for him by the Board of Aldermen on April 13, 1926, when the square itself was still on the drawing boards.

Fort George Avenue and Fort George Hill
The Namesake: Fort George, one of a chain of Revolutionary War strongpoints across upper Manhattan.

Until 1962, Fort George Hill was part of St. Nicholas Avenue.

Fort Tryon Park
The Namesake: Fort Tryon, a British strongpoint in the fighting for northern Manhattan in the Revolutionary War.

The park incorporates the site of the fort, which was named for William Tryon, the British governor of New York from 1771 to 1778, when he resigned to command British troops in the field. He was a forceful and able administrator, much admired by the city's Tories, who did not take it amiss that early in the war, for safety's sake, he spent almost a year aboard ships in the Hudson and off Sandy Hook.

Remains of Fort Tryon in 1858.

Fort Washington Avenue
The Namesake: Fort Washington, built by American Revolutionary soldiers and named for the general, but captured by British and Hessian troops in an attack that began November 16, 1776.

Part of the fort's site is incorporated in Bennett Park, just west of Fort Washington Avenue at 183rd Street. At an elevation of 267.75 feet, it is the highest natural point in Manhattan; Fort Washington Avenue used to be called, appropriately, Ridge Road.

British ships on the Hudson River by Fort Washington.

Frankfort Street

The Namesake: the birthplace in Germany of Jacob Leisler, controversial governor of New York in the late 17th century. Leisler named the street.

Leisler was the only governor of New York to be hanged. His conviction of treason was reversed by Parliament after his execution and he was "rehabilitated" with honor.

Franklin Square

The Namesake: Benjamin Franklin, "as a Testimony of the high respect entertained by this Board (the city's Common Council) for the Literary and Philosophical character of the late Doctor Benjamin Franklin."

Formerly St. George's Square, Franklin Square was renamed on March 10, 1817, some twenty-seven years after Franklin's death. With justice, the square could have been named Franklin even if Ben had never existed. A wealthy importer named Walter Franklin had an imposing house at No. 3 Cherry Street, just off the square, which served as the nation's first Executive Mansion. George Washington as President lived in it from April 23, 1789, to February 23, 1790. The house survived until 1856 and supports for Brooklyn Bridge cover its site.

Franklin Square in 1856

Franklin Street and Franklin Place

The Namesake: Benjamin Franklin.

Franklin Street was Sugar Loaf Street before January 8, 1816. Franklin Square did not get its present name until 14 months later.

Portrait of Benjamin Franklin by David Martin.

Frederick Douglass Circle

The Namesake: Frederick Augustus Washington Bailey, runaway slave who became a distinguished journalist, orator and author under the name he assumed to escape detection.

Douglass, who was half-white, crusaded for the abolition of slavery but opposed violence to achieve it and refused to join in John Brown's raid on Harpers Ferry. After the Civil War he served as marshal and recorder of deeds in the District of Columbia and then was appointed American minister to Haiti.

Frederick Douglass (ca. 1817-1895).

Frawley Circle

The Namesake: James J. Frawley, Tammany leader of the 17th Assembly District, state senator and public administrator.

The Board of Aldermen named the circle for Frawley shortly before Christmas in 1926.

Freedom Place

The Namesakes: Andrew Goodman, Michael Schwerner and James Chaney, civil rights crusaders.

The three young men were murdered in Philadelphia, Mississippi, on June 21, 1964. The street west of West End Avenue, from 66th to 70th Streets, was named for them the following year.

Front Street

The Namesake: its location in front of Water Street, which until the end of the 17th century was the city's shoreline.

Front Street and South Street were created by landfill and for a time Front Street was at the East River's edge (see Water Street).

Fulton Street

The Namesake: Robert Fulton, father of the steamship and builder of the *Clermont*, which began steamer service between New York and Albany in 1807.

An artist by profession, Fulton designed the first steam warship, *Fulton*, which was constructed at the Naval Shipyard in Brooklyn in 1814–1815. America's first nuclear submarine *Nautilus* was named for a sub built by Fulton: his had a steel hull and was propelled by sails when on the surface and by a hand-powered screw when submerged. It was the best submarine ever devised up to that time—1801—but the Navy was not interested.

Fulton's steamship Clermont, on tiles at the Fulton Street subway station.

Gansevoort Street

The Namesake: Peter Gansevoort, colonel of the 3rd New York Regiment of militia in the Revolutionary War, and later a brigadier general in the U.S. Army.

Gansevoort held off a British siege of Fort Schuyler at what is now Rome, New York and, though short of food and ammunition, spurned generous terms for surrender. His fort flew the first Stars and Stripes to see battle: the flag was contrived of ammunition bags, which were white; a captured British cloak of blue, and bits and pieces of red cloth. Before the street was named for Gansevoort, it was called Great Kiln Street, for a lime kiln sited there.

Gay Street

The Namesake: unknown, but probably for a family named Gay. An R. Gay, who lived in the Bowery, advertised a gelding for sale in a newspaper dated May 11, 1775.

The street runs through the site of a brewery owned by Wouter van Twiller, the grasping no-goodnick who succeeded Peter Minuit as Governor of New Netherland in 1633. But the name Gay Street first appears officially in the Common Council minutes for April 23, 1827, which record a health inspector's complaint against a privy belonging to one A.S. Pell, of Gay Street.

General Douglas MacArthur Plaza

The Namesake: the General of the Army who was relieved by President Truman in the Korean War for disobeying Truman's orders.

Son of a general, and a 1903 graduate of West Point, MacArthur fought in Europe in World War I, commanded all American armed forces in the Far East in World War II, and commanded all United Nations forces in Korea in 1950–51. A controversial figure, he had hordes of admirers, among whom he himself was the most dedicated.

General MacArthur at the Inchon landing, in the Korean War.

Gold Street

The Namesake: Golden Hill, a pasture that glowed with yellow flowers.

The Dutch called the flower, apparently the celandine, the *gouwe* and the area the *Gouwenberg*: the British anglicized the name to Golden Hill. Gold Street began as a path from Maiden Lane to the pasture, which covered the ground bounded by what are now William, John, Fulton and Cliff streets. The area was the scene of the Battle of Golden Hill, in which Sons of Liberty and their sympathizers clashed with British troops in 1770, several months before the so-called Boston Massacre.

Celandine (chelidonium majus).

Gouverneur Street, Gouverneur Lane and Gouverneur Slip

The Namesake: Abraham Gouverneur, a 17th-century religious refugee from France who became a leading New York merchant, political activist and ally of Jacob Leisler, the popularly chosen governor who was unjustly hanged in 1691.

After Leisler's execution, Gouverneur fled to Boston and exposed the plotting that had brought it about. In absentia, he was sentenced to death in New York, but he continued his fight and helped to win Leisler's exoneration.

Gracie Square

The Namesake Archibald Gracie, merchant, banker and advocate of free public schools, who built what is now the official residence of New York mayors.

A Scot who became a prosperous businessman in Petersburg, Virginia before settling in New York shortly after the Revolution, Gracie bought the estate of David Provoost, scion of early settlers. Gracie razed an old fort on Horn's Hook to make way for Gracie Mansion, which the young Washington Irving, whose father was a Scot, used to visit. Gracie's grandson Archibald, a Confederate general, was killed at Petersburg, where his forebear had got his start.

Gracie Mansion, with tents set up for a mayoral reception.

Gramercy Park

The Namesake: Crommessie, the Dutch for "crooked little knife," which described the shape of a brook and hill on the site.

Judith Stuyvesant, widow of Governor Peter Stuyvesant, referred to "Crommessie" in a deed she signed in 1674. A variant is *Der Krumme Zee,* for "crooked sea." The park was established in 1831 by Samuel Bulkley Ruggles, a young, successful, public-spirited lawyer who believed housing developments should be built around green open spaces held in common by the residents. The Gramercy Park area, on which he made little profit, was his pilot project.

Houses on Gramercy Park West, photographed by Berenice Abbott, 1935.

Grand Street

The Namesake: its extraordinary width, remarkable when the street was laid out before 1766.

Grand Street was the thoroughfare to Corlaers Hook, which was known also as Crown Point.

Great Jones Street

The Namesake: Samuel Jones, lawyer who, with Richard Varick, revised New York State's statutes in 1789 and became known as "the Father of the New York Bar." A Tory in the Revolution, Jones was repeatedly elected to the Assembly after the war and from 1796 to 1799 served as New York City's first comptroller, a post he had established.

Jones deeded the site of the street to the city and demanded it be named for him. But the city already had a Jones Street, named for Dr. Gardiner Jones, husband of Mrs. Samuel Jones's sister, and for a time there were two Jones Streets. Neither brother-in-law would defer to the other to end the resulting confusion and Samuel Jones finally ended the argument by suggesting: "Then make mine Great Jones Street."

Greeley Square

The Namesake: Horace Greeley, founder of the *New York Tribune*, one of the founders of the Republican Party and a leading abolitionist.

Greeley once turned down an invitation from James Gordon Bennett to join him in establishing the *New York Herald*. Long after both men were dead, the two papers were united as *The Herald-Tribune*.

Greene Street

The Namesake: Nathanael Greene, Revolutionary War general, who shared in the victory over the British at Trenton on Christmas Eve, 1776.

A Quaker-born Rhode Islander, Greene was expelled from the Society of Friends for participating in a military parade before the Revolution. He was denied a commission in a militia outfit because of a stiff knee, so he served in the ranks. During the war, he became a right-hand man to General Washington and acquired a reputation as a brilliant strategist.

Major General Nathanael Greene (1742-1786).

Greenwich Avenue and Greenwich Street

The Namesakes: roads to Greenwich Village from the city when "the Village" was out in the country. Greenwich means "Green Village," the *wich* deriving from the Saxon *wick* and the Latin *vicus* for village. The name Greenwich is mentioned in city records for the first time on March 28, 1713.

Greenwich Street was the more direct route but was so close to the Hudson that it often was flooded. So drivers usually took the longer but easier approach via Greenwich Avenue, which had been an Indian trail and then a lovers' lane.

Grove Street, Grove Court

The Namesake: gardens and groves through which the street was cut long before its present name was bestowed.

The street has had several names. In 1799, it was Columbia. Then it became Cozine, for a well-known family. After the War of 1812, it was christened Burrows, for Lieutenant William Burrows, who died when his ship, the sloop *Enterprise*, bested the British brig *Boxer*. However, Burrows was easily confused with nearby Barrow Street, and had to give way to Grove. Before the street was either Burrows or Grove, Tom Paine died there in 1809, at No. 59, which was the home of Mme. Nicholas de Bonneville. The De Bonnevilles were old friends of Paine: Nicholas de Bonneville had helped Paine after Paine's release from a French prison and Paine in turn had assisted the De Bonnevilles when they came to America.

Thomas Paine, political theorist and writer who lived for several years in France, and who died in 1809 at No. 59 Grove Street, the home of Mme. de Bonneville.

Hamill Place

The Namesake: Peter J. Hamill, who succeeded Thomas J. Foley (*see* Foley Square) as the Tammany boss in lower Manhattan after Foley's death in 1925.

The place was a nameless alley between Worth and Centre streets when it was chosen in 1936 to immortalize Hamill. "Thus the city honors the late Peter Hamill, who was a distinguished leader of the First Assembly District," said Alderman Morton Moses, chairman of the aldermanic committee on public thoroughfares, when the committee approved the street's designation.

Hamilton Place and Hamilton Terrace

The Namesake: Alexander Hamilton.

Hamilton's home, The Grange, is nearby.

Alexander Hamilton's country home, The Grange, around 1890.

Hamilton Fish Park

The Namesake: Hamilton Fish, U.S. Secretary of State during President Ulysses S. Grant's two administrations, 1869-1877.

Fish, who was born in New York City in 1808 and was graduated from Columbia College with highest honors in 1827, was elected to Congress as a Whig in 1842. He served only one term. Subsequently, he became governor of New York State for a term during which free schools were established state-wide. The state legislature, which elected U.S. senators in those days, sent him to the Senate in 1851 after a long battle in which Fish's victory was made possible only by the chance absence of two Democrats. Fish did not distinguish himself in the Senate. He became a Republican after the collapse of the Whig party but had no claim to a place in President Grant's cabinet. Fish accepted the post of Secretary of State reluctantly after initially refusing it. During his tenure, however, he successfully carried on negotiations with Britain over Civil War claims and with Spain over the insurrection in Cuba. He died in 1893.

Hon. Hamilton Fish, photographed in Mathew Brady's studio.

Hammarskjold Plaza

The Namesake: Dag Hammarskjold (1905–61), Secretary-General of the United Nations.

Hammarskjold was killed in a plane crash in Africa while on a peacemaking mission. The plaza, which abuts the UN headquarters, was named shortly after Hammarskjold's death.

Dag Hammarskjold at a press conference in 1954, a year after he became Secretary-General of the United Nations.

Hanover Square and Hanover Street

The Namesake: the House of Hanover, the German family that became Britain's sovereigns in 1714.

Like most place names related to British rule, those of Hanover Square and Hanover Street were changed in an official purge by the Common Council in 1794: the square and the street were incorporated in Pearl Street. But the changes were never enforced and Hanover Street was officially opened under that name in 1830.

Hancock Place and Hancock Square

The Namesake: General Winfield Scott Hancock.

Hero of the Battle of Gettysburg, Hancock was the Democratic nominee for the Presidency in 1880, but lost to James A. Garfield, who also had been a Civil War general.

General Winfield S. Hancock lying wounded at the Battle of Gettysburg.

Harlem River Drive

The Namesake: the Harlem River nearby.

Known originally as the Harlem River Speedway, or just The Speedway, the drive was opened on July 5, 1898, from 155th Street to Dyckman Street at 198th Street for "the driving of horses attached to light carriages." For years it was chiefly utilized by sportsmen for trotting horse trials. It became a parkway in 1915, but attracted little traffic: a count in the winter of 1917 showed only five vehicles each way on a given day. A 1918 pamphlet by Reginald Pelham Bolton, local historian and secretary of the Washington Heights Taxpayers Association, was titled *$5,000,000 Speedway, a Useless Driveway*, and indicated that the drive's abolition would save the city $14,000 a year in upkeep cost. At the 1937 suggestion of Borough President Samuel Levy, te drive was extended south to 125th Street to connect with the north end of the then projected East River Drive, now the Franklin D. Roosevelt Drive. The extension, which reshaped the Harlem River Drive between 155th and 165th Streets, isolated the segment of the old Speedway that headed inland at 165th Street and ran west of the Polo Grounds. That segment survives, bordering Colonial Houses and Polo Ground Houses.

Fast trotters on Harlem Lane, the Speedway, in a Currier and Ives etching in 1870.

Harrison Street

The Namesake: Harrison's Brewery, which operated there, close to the Hudson River, before the Revolution.

George Harrison, presumably the brewery's owner, had an estate in the area through which the street runs. His property is marked on a 1767 map of the city and the street appears on a 1797 map.

Harry Blumenstein Plaza

The Namesake: Deputy Inspector Harry Blumenstein of the New York Police Department.

The plaza, at the northwest corner of the intersection of Broome and Pitt streets, was named for Inspector Blumenstein in 1976, the year he died. A Lower East Sider by birth, Mr. Blumenstein endeared himself to the community because he spoke its languages—Chinese, Italian, Spanish and Yiddish—and understood its problems. The stationhouse of the Seventh Precinct, which he once commanded, stands at the plaza.

Haven Avenue

The Namesake: John Haven, who lived in what is now Fort Washington Park.

Haven, whose property extended to the Hudson's shore, sold out to the city in 1894.

Harry Howard Square

The Namesake: Harry Howard, a foundling born in 1822, who became head of the city's fire department in 1857.

A fireman before he was appointed chief, Howard personally saved 100 lives. He introduced the system of permanent alert in the department; as a result, fire insurance companies had to cut their rates. Howard never married because his sweetheart's parents refused to accept a foundling as a son-in-law. So Howard and his beloved lived out their lives as an engaged couple.

The city's fire department in action on Broadway in 1857, the year Harry Howard became its head.

Henderson Place

The Namesake: John C. Henderson, who built the red brick, steep-roofed houses there in 1882.

Henderson Place, a tiny enclave running north from 86th Street just west of East End Avenue, was intended by Henderson to appeal to home-buyers of "moderate means." The little street has been designated the Henderson Place Historic District by the Landmarks Preservation Commission.

Henderson Place in 1936; photo by Charles Phelphs Cushing.

Henry Hudson Parkway

The Namesake: the English sea captain and explorer who, working for the Dutch, was the first European to sail up the river that now bears his surname. The parkway parallels the river.

Hudson, who was looking for a northwesterly shortcut to the Orient, was not the first white man to visit the site of New York. But his 1609 voyage led to the city's birth: a few years after his arrival, Dutch fur traders set up shop in four huts in the vicinity of what is now 39–45 Broadway.

19th-century engraving of Henry Hudson descending the river.

Henry Street

The Namesake: Henry Rutgers (*see* Rutgers Street).

Rutgers was honored with a second street name after he donated two lots to the city as a school site. He stipulated that the school had to be built before 1811: it was completed in 1810.

Plaque commemorating the 100th anniversary of the founding of Free School No. 2 on Henry Street.

Henshaw Street

The Namesake: a neighborhood boy killed in combat in World War I.

The street was named in 1921 at the instance of Inwood Post, American Legion, but the Post's early records have been lost and even Henshaw's first name is unknown.

Herald Square

The Namesake: the Herald Building, home of *The New York Herald* before that newspaper was merged with *The New York Tribune*.

The Herald was founded by James Gordon Bennett, for whom Bennett Avenue is named.

Herald Square and the Sixth Avenue elevated, 1909. The Herald Building is in center, and Macy's at left foreground.

Hester Street

The Namesake: Hester Rynders, daughter of Jacob Leisler, the governor who was wrongly hanged for treason in 1691.

The street was named for Hester by her husband, Barnet Rynders.

Hillside Avenue

The Namesake: its topography.

The avenue climbs and descends a hill in northern Manhattan. It was officially opened in 1913.

Horatio Street

The Namesake: General Horatio Gates.

Gates was the Revolutionary commander to whom the British General Burgoyne surrendered at Saratoga. Born in England, but a Virginian for many years, Gates moved to New York in 1790 after freeing his slaves and providing for their welfare.

General Horatio Gates (1727-1806).

Houston Street

The Namesake: William Houstoun, a Georgia delegate to the Continental Congress in 1784, 1785 and 1786.

The street was named for Houstoun by Nicholas Bayard III, whose daughter Mary became Mrs. Houstoun in 1788: the couple had met while Houstoun, a member of an ancient and aristocratic Scottish family, was serving in Congress. Bayard cut the street through a tract he owned in the vicinity of Canal Street, in which he lived, and the city later extended it to include North Street, the northern border of New York's east side at the beginning of the 19th century. The current spelling of the name is a corruption: the street appears as *Houstoun* in the city's Common Council minutes for 1808 and on an official map drawn in 1811. In those years, the Texas hero Sam Houston, for whom the street is sometimes said to have been named, was an unknown teenager in Tennessee. Also mistaken is the explanation that the name derives from the Dutch words *huys* for "house" and *tuyn* for "garden."

Peale's silhouette of William Houstoun, Georgia delegate to the Constitutional Convention.

Howard Street

The Namesake: not recorded.

Howard Street originally was part of Hester Street. The Common Council renamed it in 1820: presumably a man named Howard lived there. Howard Street is not without its historic associations, though: in the Civil War, wounded soldiers convalesced at a hospital in the Soldiers' Depot at Nos. 50–52 Howard Street.

Hubert Street

The Namesake: Hubert Van Wagonen, a vestryman of Trinity Church.

Van Wagonen, a dealer in iron, was honored when Trinity deeded the land for the street to the city.

Hubert Van Wagonen.

Hudson Street

The Namesake: the river close by.

The street was laid out before 1797, and Trinity Church ceded the land for it to the city in 1808.

Indian Road

The Namesakes: the Weekquaeskeeks, an Indian tribe that included some of New York's earliest commuters; living as far north as Irvington, the tribesmen walked down to New Amsterdam with loads of beaver skins.

Formerly known as Isham Avenue, Indian Road was named in 1911 after traces of the Indians' settlement there were uncovered in Isham Park (*see* Isham Park and Isham Street).

Dutch traders and Indians at Manhattan.

Irving Place

The Namesake: Washington Irving, the writer and diplomat.

Samuel B, Ruggles, who conceived and built Gramercy Park, laid out Irving Place in 1831 and gave it its name. Irving at the time was at the peak of his literary career.

Washington Irving and his literary contemporaries.

Jackson Street

The Namesake: Andrew Jackson, President of the United States from 1829 to 1837.

Jackson died in 1845 and the street, formerly Walnut Street, was renamed for him several years later.

Andrew Jackson, seventh President of the United States, (1829-1837).

Jacobus Place

The Namesake: Jacobus Dyckman, one of the sponsors of the free bridge built across the Harlem River at 225th Street in 1759 to frustrate the toll collectors on the King's Bridge.

Jacobus ran the Dyckman Tavern until 1769. The place named for him was not officially laid out, though, until 1892. One historian of the city contends the place was named for David Schenck Jacobus, an engineer who was born in New Jersey in 1862 and was a professor of engineering at the Stevens Institute of Technology.

James Street

The Namesake: James Desbrosses, who operated a distillery on the East River shore in the 1700s.

Desbrosses Street (*q.v.*) was named for another member of the family, Elias.

Isham Park and Isham Street

The Namesakes: the Isham family who lived there.

Mrs. Henry Osborn Taylor (née Julia Isham) and her aunt Flora E. Isham gave the land for the park to the city in 1912.

James J. Walker Park

The Namesake: "Jimmy" Walker, mayor of New York, 1926-1932.

Urbane, dapper, witty and successful as a songwriter ("Will You Love Me in December as You Do in May?") "Jimmy" Walker epitomized New York sophistication in the "Roaring Twenties." He drove a $17,000 Duesenberg, the provenance of which was obscure. He loved jazz, boxing, nightclubs, speakeasies and the company of beautiful actresses—not necessarily in that order—and was as highly regarded in Park Avenue duplexes as he was in Madison Square Garden. As mayor—according to Warren Moscow, who was a City Hall reporter in Walker's day and later rose to high rank in the Wagner administration—Walker used to visit City Hall only a couple of days a week, arriving at 3 p.m. after having arisen at noon from his luxurious hotel bed in which his bedmate was not his wife Jane.

But, says Moscow, Walker had the keenest mind ever dedicated to New York politics, and often solved problems as he raced upstairs from his office—or his hangover room beneath the office—to the Board of Estimate. Example: European shipping companies were building trans-Atlantic liners that would be 200 feet too long for New York's 800 foot piers, and federal navigation regulations forbade the piers' extension in the Hudson. "Then cut back 200 feet into the shoreline," Walker said off-handedly. Walker, who was born in 1881 at 110 Leroy Street and grew up at 6 St. Luke's Place—which remained his official home—had written one-act plays and had played semi-pro baseball for Hoboken before his election to the New York State Assembly in 1909, three years before he was admitted to the bar. After five years as an assemblyman and protege of "Al" Smith, he spent six years in the State Senate, where he fathered liberal social welfare legislation and became minority leader. Tammany Hall chose him to run for mayor in 1925. He won and his first term in office had among its achievements the improvement of the park and transportation systems. For a second term, he defeated Fiorello H. LaGuardia—who was making his first attempt to become mayor—by half a million votes. But a relatively minor scandal in the magistrates' courts led in 1931 to a legislative investigation of the city and Walker was unable to account, among other things, for $1 million in bank deposits made by his accountant, Russell T. Sherwood. Faced with removal from office, Walker resigned September 1, 1932, was divorced, and married the actress Betty Compton, who had been a long-time companion. The newlyweds spent several years abroad, and when they returned it became evident that New York could forgive "Jimmy" Walker anything: he remained as popular as he had ever been. His old political antagonist, LaGuardia, appointed him in 1940 to be impartial chairman of the garment industry, a post he held for four years. Then he became president of Majestic Records—and was back in the music business where he had first achieved success. When he was fatally stricken by a blood clot in his still lively brain on November 18, 1946, hundreds of admirers tried to get in to see him and thousands more clogged the hospital's telephone lines with anxious calls.

Major "Jimmy" Walker, tossing the first baseball of the 1932 season.

Jeannette Park

The Namesake: *Jeannette*, luckless flagship of an 1879-1881 expedition to the Arctic.

The expedition was sponsored by James Gordon Bennett, Jr., of the New York Herald, whose daughter was named Jeannette. The ship, skippered by a U.S. Navy lieutenant-commander, was lost with her crew, but the men's bodies were recovered and returned to New York, where a mass funeral was held on February 23, 1884. The state legislature named the park shortly thereafter, on April 2, 1884. Jeannette Park constitutes 7/10 of an acre at 55 Water Street and is partly occupied by a Uris Company building: the city leased the land to the company for 99 years with the requirement that the company maintain the park.

Jefferson Street

The Namesake: Thomas Jefferson, President of the United States, 1801-1809.

Before the street was named for Jefferson, it was called Washington Street.

Thomas Jefferson, third President (1801-1809) of the United States, portrait by R. Peale.

John Street

The Namesake: John Harperding or Haberdinck, a wealthy shoemaker during Dutch possession of the city.

Jane Street

The Namesake: the road to the house of a man named Jaynes, at No. 81.

Jaynes' house, built in 1750, survived until 1890. After his duel with Aaron Burr, Alexander Hamilton died there, when it was the country house of the Bayard family.

Jay Street

The Namesake: John Jay, first Chief Justice of the United States, 1789-1795.

Descendant of a late 17th-century Huguenot immigrant named Augustus Jay, John Jay worked with Alexander Hamilton and James Madison on drafting the Constitution. Jay served as governor of New York from 1795 until his retirement in 1801; he had been elected to the post while in England, where he negotiated the controversial Jay Treaty, an attempt to settle commerce and navigation rights between the two countries.

Harperding-Haberdinck owned the land which John Street occupies.

John Street in 1768, painted by Joseph Smith.

Jersey Street

The Namesake: undetermined

Jersey Street once was called Columbian Alley, also for reasons undetermined.

Jones Alley

The Namesake: Great Jones Street, to which the alley runs.

(*See* Great Jones Street)

Jones Street

The Namesake: Dr. Gardiner Jones, who laid out the street in 1794.

One-block-long Jones Street is not to be confused with two-block-long Great Jones Street, named for Samuel Jones, the doctor's brother-in-law (they married sisters).

Jumel Place and Jumel Terrace

The Namesake: Jumel Mansion, home of Stephen Jumel, a wine importer of charm, wealth and acuity, who is best remembered as the first husband of the rapacious beauty who married Aaron Burr when Burr was in his eighties.

The mansion was built by Roger Morris and used by George Washington as his headquarters in the Battle of Harlem Heights. (Washington cast admiring eyes on Mrs. Morris.) Morris, a Tory, lost the property after the Revolution and the house became a tavern in 1787. Jumel, a handsome, giant Frenchman who arrived in New York in 1795 from rebellion-swept Haiti, bought the place in 1810 for his wife and former mistress, Elizabeth (Betsey) Bowen, and there the Jumels entertained Jerome Bonaparte and the Duc de Talleyrand, whom they had known in Paris. But most of New York society raised its eyebrows at mention of Betsey and snubbed the Jumels' invitations. During Stephen Jumel's absence in France, Betsey wangled a power of attorney from her husband and made the property hers. Jumel fell off a wagon—literally—and died in 1832; Betsey married Aaron Burr the following year. The house is now a museum.

The scandalous and once beautiful Betsey Bowen, Mme. Stephen Jumel (1775-1865).

Kenmare Street

The Namesake: Kenmare, a village in Ireland.

"Big Tim" Sullivan, a turn-of-the-century Tammany leader on the Lower East Side, had the street named for his mother's birthplace.

King Street

The Namesake: Rufus King, a member of the Continental Congress from Massachusetts and a Revolutionary War soldier who later served as New York's first U.S. senator and as minister to Britain. In 1804 and 1808 he was the Federalist candidate for the vice presidency.

King moved to New York from Massachusetts in 1788. One of his sons became governor of New York, another was president of Columbia College.

Kingsbridge Avenue

The Namesake: the King's Bridge across the Harlem River.

The bridge was named for England's King William III, the Dutch-born Prince of Orange who ascended to the English throne with his English wife, Mary, in 1689. The name was bestowed by Frederick Philipse, to whom William had given permission for construction of the bridge and collection of tolls.

King's Bridge over Spuyten Duyvil Creek in 1856.

Lafayette Street

The Namesake: Marie Joseph Paul Yves Roch Gilbert du Motier, Marquis de La Fayette.

A hero of the American Revolution and a leader in the French Revolution, La Fayette was given a tremendous and touching welcome when he returned to New York for a visit in 1824. Lafayette Street was originally Lafayette Place, a three-block-long, broad and leafy dead-end street on which John Jacob Astor's son William B. erected mansions for himself and his sisters. (Lafayette Place opened onto Astor Place, which had been renamed for John Jacob.) Then the city cut through the dead end, lengthened Lafayette Place and made it the now nondescript thoroughfare that is Lafayette Street.

The Marquis de Lafayette directing troops against the British fortifications at Yorktown.

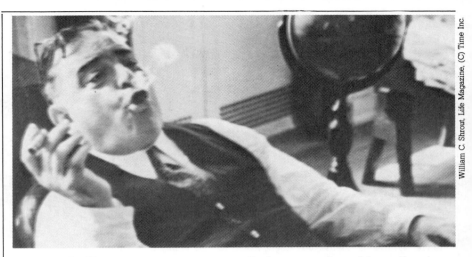

La Guardia Place

The Namesake: Fiorello Henry La Guardia, the most rambunctious and most colorful mayor in New York's history and the first one in modern times to be elected to three consecutive terms (1934— 1945). He was the first American of Italian ancestry to attain such high office and the first of Jewish ancestry— his mother was a Jew— to serve New York as mayor.

Five feet two inches tall, henshaped (as *Time* described him), and as feisty as a fighting cock, La Guardia was a rare fowl among politicians. He was normally a Republican, but he won more support, on and off, from New Deal Democrats, Socialists, Progressives, American Laborites and Liberals than he did in his own party. He is best remembered for racing firemen to fires and for reading the Sunday comics over the radio during a newspaper strike but he ran the city with rare honesty and efficiency. His whole career differed greatly from that of other New York politicians. Born in Greenwich Village's Varick Street in 1882 to young immigrants, La Guardia grew up in Arizona, where his father was an army bandmaster. His father died in the Spanish American War of eating tainted beef supplied to the troops by crooked meat packers, and La Guardia became a lifelong foe of fraud and corruption. After his father's death, he got a job in the U.S. Consulate in Budapest— where his mother is buried in the Jewish Cemetery— and shortly was transferred to the consulate in Trieste as interpreter. (He spoke Yiddish, Italian, German, French and assorted Croatian dialects, which he later put to good use in politics.) At 20, he became the American consul in Fiume, but after a row over a matter of principle, he returned to America. Working by day as an interpreter at Ellis Island, he studied law at night, and in 1916 was elected to Congress as a Republican in what had been an impregnably Democratic district. With America's entry into World War I in April, 1917, he quit Congress to enlist. Rejected by the army as too small to soldier, he learned to fly, joined the air corps, and became an ace on the Italian front. He was elected President of the Board of Aldermen in 1919 and in 1923 returned to Congress where he remained until his election as mayor in 1934. When he died in 1947, after abjuring a fourth term in City Hall, the signal 5-5-5-5 sounded in every firehouse in New York. It was the traditional tribute to a fireman killed in the line of duty.

Major Fiorello La Guardia at his desk.

William C. Shrout, Life Magazine, (C) Time Inc.

Laight Street

The Namesake: William Laight, a prominent merchant and member of the patriotic Committee of 100 before the Revolutionary War.

Laight remained in New York during the British occupation, but was not, as friends put it, "neutral in opinion." He was a vestryman of Trinity Church, and the Trinity vestry had the street named for him.

La Salle Street

The Namesake: Jean Baptiste de la Salle, the 17th-century French priest who founded the Christian Brothers. He was canonized in 1900.

La Salle Street was formerly part of 125th Street. Manhattan College, organized by the Christian Brothers in 1853, was nearby at 131st Street and Broadway.

Laurel Hill Terrace

The Namesake: Laurel Hill, which was covered with laurel bushes.

The name Laurel Hill predates the Revolutionary War.

Sweet Bay (Laurus nobilis), the true laurel.

Lenox Avenue

The Namesakes: the Lenox family that established the Lenox Library, now long a part of the New York Public Library.

The family's fortune was founded by Robert Lenox, who was born in Scotland in 1759, arrived in New York as a boy, and became a merchant and real estate operator. A historian of the Chamber of Commerce of the State of New York, of which Robert was president from 1826 to 1839, wrote of him: "Such was his prudence and sagacity that it is not believed there was a year during the whole period of the actual mercantile life, in which he did not find his property greater at the close than it had been at the commencement." One of his sagacious deals was the purchase in 1818 of 30 acres between Fourth and Fifth avenues and 68th and 71st streets. After his death at 80, in 1839, his son James donated a site for the Lenox Library on Fifth Avenue from 70th to 71st Street.

The Lenox Library on Fifth Avenue at 70th Street.

Lenox Terrace Place

The Namesake: Lenox Avenue.

The little street, site of Lenox Terrace Houses, lies between Lenox and Fifth Avenues and runs from 134th to 135th streets. Newly created, it was named in 1961.

Leonard Street

The Namesake: Leonard Lispenard, whose father Anthony owned the Lispenard Meadows through which several streets were cut.

Anthony Lispenard named three streets for his sons, Leonard, Anthony and Thomas. Anthony Street was renamed Worth Street to honor Major General William Jenkins Worth, a hero of the War with Mexico, 1848.

Leroy Street

The Namesake: Jacob Leroy, alderman and head of Jacob Le Roy & Sons, a firm of world-wide traders, based there from the end of the 18th century.

The Le Roy firm made huge profits running the British blockade during the War of 1812. The playground on Leroy Street was a graveyard until the 1890s. When the playground was built, a gravestone dug up there gave rise to a curious legend. The gravestone bore the inscription *Leroy*—nothing more—and because the name means "*the King*" in French the story spread that the stone marked the grave of Louis Charles, son of King Louis XVI and Marie Antoinette. Louis Charles supposedly died in a French prison at the age of 10, after the execution of his parents, but there was some evidence that he had been smuggled to freedom and had long survived outside France. And he died, the story went, in Greenwich Village. Alas, the name Leroy Street appears on a map made in 1807, too early to support the tale.

Blockade of ships during the War of 1812.

Lexington Avenue

The Namesake: the Battle of Lexington.

Lexington and Madison Avenues were not included in the 1811 plan of the city, which established the grid system for streets and avenues. By 1832, additional avenues became necessary, and Samuel Ruggles, lawyer and real estate developer who fathered Gramercy Park, opened Lexington Avenue through his own property and petitioned the city to name it for the military clash at the start of the Revolution.

The Battle of Lexington, as depicted by a French artist and engraver.

Leyden Street

The Namesake: Leyden University in The Netherlands.

Adriaen van der Donck, the city's first lawyer, received his law degree at Leyden.

Liberty Place

The Namesake: nearby Liberty Street.

Lying between Nassau Street and Broadway, Liberty Place runs from Liberty Street to Maiden Lane. It dates to the late 17th century, when it was known as Little Green Street.

Liberty Street

The Namesake: emancipation of the American colonies from British rule.

The street had been called Crown Street, a name the city fathers did not get around to changing until 1794.

Publications from 1773.

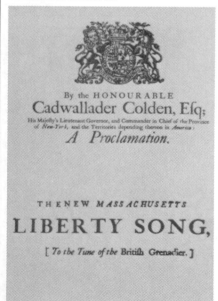

Lt. William Tighe Triangle

The Namesake: a resident of the neighborhood, in northern Manhattan, who was killed in World War II.

The little open space was named in 1950.

Ludlow Street

The Namesake: Lieutenant Augustus C. Ludlow, a naval hero of the War of 1812 to whom Captain James Lawrence said: "Don't give up the ship."

Ludlow, 21, took command of the frigate *Chesapeake* when Lawrence was mortally wounded in battle with the British ship *Shannon* off Boston Harbor. His *actual* orders from Lawrence were: "Tell the men to fire faster and not give up the ship. Fight her till she sinks." But Ludlow himself was hit fatally and the two men are buried in one grave at Trinity Church.

The death of Captain Lawrence on the frigate Chesapeake.

Lillian Wald Drive

The Namesake: Lillian D. Wald, the Ohio-born social worker who founded the Henry Street Settlement.

Miss Wald died in 1940.

Lispenard Street

The Namesake: Anthony Lispenard, a religious refugee from France in the 18th century, who became an alderman, an assemblyman, and treasurer of King's College.

A man of property, Lispenard joined forces with the Rutgers family by marrying Alice Rutgers in 1741. The street runs through what was once the Lispenard Meadows.

Little West Twelfth Street

The Namesake: its location.

Little West Twelfth Street runs from Ninth to Tenth Avenue and is physically separated from the longer Twelfth Street proper.

MacDougal Street and MacDougal Alley

The Namesake: Alexander McDougall (whose father spelled it MacDougal), anti-British agitator in colonial days and Revolutionary War commander.

McDougall came to America from the Hebrides as a child and as a young man skippered a British privateer for seven years before settling down as a New York merchant. He was a founder of the underground Sons of Liberty, and a pamphlet he wrote denouncing British restrictions on trade landed him in jail in 1770. Refusing bail, he advertised that he was "at home" to callers in prison, and had so many that he had to see visitors by appointment only. In the war, he first served as colonel of the First New York City Guard Regiment, rose to major general, and succeeded Benedict Arnold in command of the defenses of West Point. He represented New York in the Continental Congress, later became first president of the Bank of New York, and was a state senator when he died in 1786, at the age of 53.

Macombs Place

The Namesake: Alexander Macomb, a hero of the War of 1812, who lived at the site that bears his name.

Macomb, commanding a greatly outnumbered force, had held Plattsburg, the American army's northern headquarters, against a siege by 14,000 British troops. He achieved victory by a ruse: he secretly rearranged roads near the town and the British, following one that Macomb's men had just opened, marched into the Americans' field of fire. Macomb's Dam Park, at Jerome Avenue and 161st Street, is the site of a dam built by his son Robert to utilize the flow of the Harlem River for operating a mill. His neighbors angrily tore down the dam in 1838 to open the river to shipping. The Macombs Dam Bridge crosses the river there now.

Bass fishing at Macomb's Dam on the Harlem River, Lithograph by N. Currier.

Magaw Place

The Namesake: Robert Magaw, a Philadelphia lawyer and Revolutionary War colonel who fought in the Battle of Harlem Heights.

Magaw, who had marched a Pennsylvania regiment to New York, commanded Fort Washington during the British attack on northern Manhattan. When the American troops ran out of ammunition, Magaw finally surrendered and was taken prisoner with 2700 men, most of whom were from other regiments and had fled to the fort.

Broadway at Madison Square, 1893.

Madison Street and Madison Square

The Namesake: President James Madison.

Madison Street was named in 1826, ten years before Madison Avenue. The street had been Bancker Street, for a Rutgers son-in-law, but the neighborhood had deteriorated and the Banckers asked that their name be removed.

Madison Avenue

The Namesake: President James Madison, who died the year the avenue was opened, 1836.

Like Lexington Avenue, Madison Avenue was not part of the city's 1811 grid plans. It too was created at the urging of Samuel Ruggles, the founder of Gramercy Park.

James Madison.

Maher Circle

The Namesake: a neighborhood boy killed in World War I.

Like a number of other World War I heroes whom the city intended to immortalize (see Henshaw and Staff streets), Maher is commemorated only by his surname: no data on him have been found in city archives.

Mangin Street

The Namesake: Joseph Francis Mangin, appointed city surveyor in 1795, co-designer of the present City Hall in 1802.

A refugee from the French Revolution, Mangin prepared an official map of New York in 1797 in collaboration with Casimir T. Goerck. For his work on the plan for City Hall, he shared a $300 prize with John McComb, Jr.

Plan of the City of New York published in 1803.

Maiden Lane

The Namesake: a footpath beside a pebbly brook that ran from Nassau Street to the East River.

Although the path (*Maagde Paetje* is Dutch for Maiden Lane) was a favorite strolling place for lovers, the name had a less romantic origin: the gentle grassy slope of the brook's bank provided an ideal spot for washing and bleaching clothes, a chore assigned to young girls in most families.

Broadway and Maiden Lane around 1885.

Manhattan Avenue and Manhattan Place.
The Namesake: Guess!

Manhattan is an Indian name for which supposed translations abound. Among the more fanciful is "the place where we all got drunk," which refers to an alleged drinking party Henry Hudson arranged for Indian shipboard visitors. But the carefully kept log of Hudson's *Half Moon* makes no mention of this. Another interpretation is "People of the Whirlpool"—a reference, no doubt, to Hell Gate. More persuasive is this: in the language of the Delaware Indians, *manah* meant "*island*" and *atin* meant "*hill*". The island's Indians called themselves *Manahatta*.

Marble Hill Avenue and Marble Hill Place
The Namesake: Marble Hill, a high rock in a 52-acre community that is physically part of The Bronx and the only segment of Manhattan that is on the continent's mainland. The name was coined in 1891 by Darius C. Crosby: the Indians had called the area "The Glistening Place."

The community was severed from Manhattan physically when the shallow, winding portion of the Harlem River was shifted and deepened in 1895 to make it navigable. The river's old course was left dry and the present channel was blasted through rock. But the old course remained the boundary between the boroughs and the borough presidents of Manhattan and The Bronx wrangle sporadically over who should run the place.

Marcus Garvey Park, formerly Mt. Morris Park
The Namesake: Marcus Garvey, the ill-starred black leader who attempted to organize a Back-to-Africa mass migration earlier in this century.

Born in Jamaica in the West Indies about 1880, Garvey came to this country in 1914 after a year of travel, he said, in Europe. In Harlem, he organized the Universal Negro Improvement Association, the African Community League, the Order of the Nile, the Black Cross Nurses and the Universal African Legion. But his major interest was in leading his fellow blacks back to Africa, on the soil of which he apparently never had set foot. To that end, he proclaimed himself Emperor of the Kingdom of Africa and once appeared before the League of Nations as representative of the "black peoples of the world." He also dubbed himself "Sir Provisional President of Africa," and bestowed the titles of prince, princess, baron, duke, earl, viscount and knight on his followers, whom he gained in Harlem and elsewhere through his fiery lectures. For transportation to Africa, he founded the Black Star Steamship Line and the Black Star Steamship Company, in which he offered shares at $5 each to 5,000 fellow blacks gathered in the old Madison Square Garden. The companies acquired two vessels, *Yarmouth* and Colonel Henry Huddleston Rogers' yacht *Kanawha*. *Yarmouth's* first assignment was to carry $3 million worth of liquor from Brooklyn to Cuba to get it out of the country before Prohibition became effective January 15, 1920. But *Yarmouth's* crew sampled the cargo too generously and the vessel had to put into Norfolk, where ship and liquor were seized by the Feds. *Kanawha,* on her first voyage for Garvey, also put into Norfolk, where her skipper rammed a pier so hard that a boiler exploded and *Kanawha*, too, was a total loss. Garvey's misfortunes were compounded when he was convicted of mail fraud in connection with one of the shipping companies and was sent, in February 1925, to Atlantic Penitentiary. The sentence was commuted in 1927 so that he could be deported to Jamaica. His remaining years were spent in obscurity and he died in London on June 10, 1940. Mt. Morris Park was renamed for him in the 1970s in recognition of his efforts on behalf of his race.

Marcus Garvey in New York.

Margaret Corbin Drive

The Namesake: Margaret Cochran Corbin, a heroine of the Revolution.

A 25-year-old Pennsylvania frontierswoman, Margaret stood by her Virginian husband John in the patriot forces. She took his place behind a cannon when he was killed on November 16, 1776 in the Battle of Fort Washington and was gravely wounded herself. After the war she settled in what is now Highland Falls, New York. Tart of tongue, short of temper, careless of dress, and employed as a domestic servant, she nevertheless was addressed always as "Captain Molly." She died in 1800 of her battle injuries and was buried in Highland Park in a grave marked only by a tree. In 1926 the Daughters of the American Revolution had her remains exhumed and re-interred in the Post Cemetery at West Point — one of the very few women to rest in the warriors section there. Margaret Corbin Drive, which is close by the scene of her exploit, was named for her in June 1977.

Tablet in memory of Margaret Corbin, in Holyrood Church.

Marketfield Street

The Namesake: *Marcktveldt*, the Dutch designation for the first live-stock market, held in the vicinity of what is now Battery Park.

Opened in 1638, the market was shut down in 1647.

Market Street and Market Slip

The Namesake: Catherine Market, established in 1786 between Catherine Street and what is now Market Street.

Until 1813, Market Street was known as George Street. Market Slip, an extension of Market Street, was a port of entry for the produce sold in Catherine Market.

Martin Square

The Namesake: undetermined, but presumably a neighborhood resident who was killed in World War I.

The square was named April 1, 1925.

McCarthy Square

The Namesake: Private First Class Bernard Joseph McCarthy of the Marines, killed on Guadalcanal in August, 1942.

The little square, bounded by Seventh Avenue, Charles Street and Waverly Place, was named June 5, 1943.

McKenna Square

The Namesake: undetermined.

Mercer Street

The Namesake: Hugh Mercer, a Revolutionary War officer killed in the preliminaries of the Battle of Princeton in 1777.

A Scottish-born surgeon, Mercer became a brigadier general in the American army and it was he who advised General Washington to undertake the march on Princeton that resulted in the defeat of part of Lord Cornwallis' forces.

Milligan Place

The Namesake: Samuel Milligan, who bought farmland there in 1799 and hired Aaron D. Patchin, his future son-in-law, to survey it.

Milligan Place and nearby Patchin Place, which also was part of Milligan's property, were built up in 1848–49 with boarding houses to accommodate the Basques employed in the kitchen and dining room of the long famous, now defunct Brevoort Hotel.

Milligan Place in 1936, photographed by Berenice Abbott.

Mill Lane

The Namesake: a 1628 mill in which bark was ground for use by tanners. The mill was powered by horses walking in a circle.

The city's first formal religious services under an ordained minister were held in 1628 in the mill's huge loft and Peter Stuyvesant surrendered New Amsterdam to the British at 8 a.m. of August 29, 1664, at the mill. The lane, which runs from South William Street to Stone Street, is a remnant of Mill Street, the mill's site. Mill Street's name was changed to South William Street.

Minetta Lane, Minetta Place, Minetta Street

The Namesake: Minetta Brook, which rose in the long-since-leveled Zantberg (Sand Hill) range near 23rd Street and emptied into the Hudson near Charlton Street. The brook still flows beneath Greenwich Village streets and houses.

Minetta Brook was known to the Dutch as Mintje Kill, for small stream. *Min* in Dutch means "little," and *tje* is a diminutive. British tongues turned *mintje* into Minetta. The vicinity of the brook was the home of New Amsterdam's first free black farmers, who were given land there in the 1640s when the Dutch released them from slavery. The Indians and the Dutch fished the Minetta for brook trout and as late as the 1840s the merchant A.T. Stewart—John Wanamaker's predecessor—and the famous Dr. Valentine Mott drew their household water supply from it.

Monroe Street

The Namesake: James Monroe, fifth president of the United States.

Monroe lived at 349 the Bowery during his vice-presidency, and later in Prince Street. He died in New York and was buried in the Marble Cemetery in Second Street between First and Second avenues. Later the body was reinterred in Monroe's native Virginia.

Mitchell Place

The Namesake: William Mitchell, distinguished 19th-century New York jurist, and a member of the bar for 63 years.

An honors graduate from Columbia and the editor of an American version of *Blackstone's Commentaries* (which he was too modest to sign), Mitchell served as presiding justice of the State Supreme Court and as a member of the Court of Appeals. After his retirement in 1857, he remained so highly regarded that litigants took cases to him for trial privately. Mitchell Place was named in 1871. Mitchell died in 1886, at age 85.

Moore Street

The Namesake: Moor Street, off which ships anchored in the East River. The custom house stood nearby and a pier was built in front of it.

Moore Street is no relative of North Moore Street, which is on the other side of Manhattan, and which is named for a bishop. (Moore Street's name sometimes is attributed, almost certainly erroneously, to a Colonel John Moore, a Manhattan resident about 1735, who bought a fire engine that was kept in the second City Hall in Wall Street when the engine was not in use.

Mitchell Square

The Namesake: John Purroy Mitchel (with one l), youngest mayor in New York's history when he was elected in 1913, age 34. He died bizarrely after one term in office.

Son of a New York City fire marshal who had served on Stonewall Jackson's staff in the Civil War, Mitchel was graduated with honors from New York Law School in 1901 and five years later was famous: an investigation he had been appointed to conduct brought about the removal of Manhattan Borough President John F. Ahearn and of Bronx Borough President Louis Haffen. Anti-Tammany forces elected Mitchel president of the Board of Aldermen in 1909 and mayor four years later, but his reputed snobbishness cost him re-election in 1917. With the first World War raging, Mitchel enlisted in the army aviation corps. Flying solo near the end of his training at Gerstner Field, Lake Charles, Louisiana, on July 6, 1918, Mitchel fell out of his plane at 500 feet and plunged to his death. His safety belt was found unfastened.

Montefiore Square

The Namesake: The Montefiore Home for Chronic Diseases, which stood at 138th and 139th streets and Broadway. Established in 1884 in East 84th Street near Carl Schurz Park as the Montefiore Home for Incurable Invalids, the institution adopted a more sensitive name when it moved to upper Broadway. It is now the Montefiore Hospital and Medical Center in The Bronx.

The names of the square and the hospital actually commemorate Sir Moses Haim Montefiore, an Italian-born (1784) Jewish philanthropist, London stockbroker and brother-in-law of Nathan Mayer Rothschild. Having amassed a fortune before middle age, Montefiore devoted the rest of his 101 years of life to fighting for the rights of his fellow Jews, tackling the Czar of Russia, the Vatican, Mohammed Ali, the strongman of Egypt and the Middle East, and Abdul Aziz, the Sultan of the Turkish Empire. After Montefiore's election as sheriff of the City of London, he was knighted by Queen Victoria, who later made him a baronet. Strictly orthodox in worship, Sir Moses maintained a synagogue on his estate and attended services twice daily. The original Montefiore Home was named for him on his 100th birthday.

Morningside Avenue

The Namesake: the eastern, or morning, side of a rocky elevation occupied by Morningside Park.

Until 1890, the avenue was part of Ninth Avenue: it was renamed at the same time that the longer segment of Ninth Avenue extending south to 59th Street was rechristened Columbus Avenue.

Morningside Drive

The Namesake: Morningside Park.

The drive serves as the park's western boundary.

Montgomery Street

The Namesake: Brigadier General Richard Montgomery, who led New York troops in a midnight attempt to storm Quebec on December 31, 1775. Montgomery and two aides were killed by artillery fire.

Montgomery's unlikely last words are supposed to have been: "Men of New York, you will not fear to follow where your general leads." But when he fell, the troops turned tails and fled. The general is buried in St. Paul's Chapel.

The death of General Montgomery, engraved from a painting by John Trumbull.

Morton Street

The Namesake: Jacob Morton, a prominent lawyer and part-time soldier in the early 1800s.

Morton enjoyed the title of general as commander of the 1st Division of the New York militia, a post he held for 30 years. Morton's wife was the beautiful Catherine Ludlow and the couple lived in the 26-room Ludlow mansion at 9—11 State Street. Originally, Morton's name was borne by what is now Clarkson Street, but in 1807 the Common Council moved the name two blocks north to make a place of honor for Matthew Clarkson (*see* Clarkson Street), who outranked Morton in the militia.

Catherine Ludlow Morton, painted by S.F.B. Morse

Morris Street

The Namesake: Gouverneur Morris, member of the Continental Congress and later ambassador to France.

Morris was one of the city commissioners, named in 1807, who laid out Manhattan's streets on the grid plan. Before Morris Street was given his name in 1829, it was part of Beaver Street.

Dr. Valentine Mott.

Mott Street

The Namesake: Joseph Mott, a prosperous butcher before the Revolution: Mott Street appears on a city map drawn in 1776.

Joseph Mott's tavern, at what is now 143rd Street and Eighth Avenue, served as Washington's headquarters on September 15, 1775, before the General moved into the Morris (now Jumel) Mansion. Motts long were leading citizens. The first Mott here, Adam, arrived in 1635 from England, where the name originally had been de la Motte. Jacob Mott, a great-grandson of Adam, was a wealthy merchant who served as an alderman from 1804 to 1810 and as deputy mayor under DeWitt Clinton. Two decades later, Dr. Valentine Mott, who was attached to Bellevue Hospital, was one of the city's best known and best liked surgeons.

Mulberry Street

The Namesake: a mulberry grove on the site.

The street appears on a map drawn in 1767.

Mulry Square

The Namesake: Thomas W. Mulry, banker and Greenwich Villager active in Roman Catholic charities.

One of fourteen children and a native New Yorker, Mulry became president of the Emigrant Industrial Savings Bank and of the St. Vincent de Paul Society, of which he was a founder. When he died in 1916, age 61, 110 priests assisted in the services in St. Patrick's Cathedral and the overflow of mourners blocked Fifth Avenue traffic. The square, which Mulry's home at 10 Perry Street overlooked, was dedicated on June 27, 1920; 5,000 villagers, as well as Achbishop (later Cardinal) Patrick J. Hayes and Mayor John F. Hylan attended the ceremonies, the Police Glee Club sang and the Fire Department Band played.

Nagle Avenue

The Namesake: Jan Nagel, a soldier in Dutch service who became a wealthy landowner and real estate speculator at Manhattan's northern end.

A far-sighted investor, Nagel plunged jointly with Jan Dyckman to acquire 74 acres, which they leased to a farmer in 1677 for two hens a year for seven years: wisely, they were more interested in the future than in the immediate income.

Nassau Street

The Namesake: the House of Orange-Nassau, which dates back to Charlemagne and which reigns in The Netherlands. (The principality of Orange is now part of France and Nassau part of Germany.) The street's name was bestowed in honor of the male half of the team of William and Mary who ascended the English throne in 1689. William was a scion of the Orange-Nassau family. There used to be an Orange Street as well, but it was renamed Baxter Street because it had fallen into disrepute.

William—King William III of England—got his share of the throne and all of the power by a show of Dutch firmness. (His father had been stadtholder of the Dutch Republic.) His English wife Mary was invited to become Queen—though she was not next in line of succession—when her father James II fled his dissentious country; William, whose army—also by invitation—had helped to precipitate Jame's flight, was informed that he could be Prince Consort. William said, in effect, "No way." If his wife was to be Queen, he would be King. He won. And thereafter, he did all the ruling. His claim to the throne, though, had more than *chutzpah* as its base: William was a grandson of the beheaded Charles I.

New Street

The Namesake: its status as the first street opened in the city after the British took over New Amsterdam.

North Moore Street

The Namesake: Benjamin Moore, simultaneously rector of Trinity Church, Episcopalian Bishop of New York and President of Columbia College from 1801 to 1811.

Moore, a Tory, headed King's College, Columbia's predecessor, as president *pro tem* from 1775 to 1784; the previous president, Myles Cooper, also a Tory, had fled. The bishop was the father of Clement C. Moore, who wrote "'Twas the night before Christmas . . ." The street is called North Moore to distinguish it from Moore Street.

Nathan D. Perlman Place

The Namesake: the four-term Manhattan congressman (1920–1927), justice of the Court of Special Sessions and New York State attorney general, who was active in philanthropic work as well.

Polish-born, Perlman was a 1905 graduate of CCNY. He died in 1952.

Norfolk Street

The Namesake: the English county of that name.

Old Broadway

The Namesake: a bend in the road.

A fragment of the old Bloomingdale Road, Old Broadway was part of Broadway until Broadway was straightened at that point, leaving Old Broadway on its own.

Old Slip

The Namesake: a long-since filled-in slip for ships.

The slip dated back to 1691. The 90-ton brig *Betsy*, built here in 1792 and a pioneer of the vast American merchant fleet of the 19th century, sailed out of Old Slip to become the first ship to carry the American flag around the world. Captain Edmund Fanning commanded her. Previously, American imports and exports had moved in British vessels.

Oliver Street

The Namesake: Oliver de Lancey, colonial politician and soldier.

Oliver de Lancey was the youngest son of Étienne de Lancey and the brother of James de Lancey, for whom Delancey Street is named. A prosperous merchant, he served as an alderman, as an assemblyman, and as a pre-Revolution councilman. In the French and Indian Wars, he raised and commanded troops in the Ticonderoga campaign of 1758. (Marinus Willett, for whom Willett Street is named, was one of his officers.) In the Revolution, he remained loyal to King George III and served as a brigadier general in the British army. As a result, his property was confiscated and he died in exile, in 1785.

New York under the British flag, in a view of the Battery and Fort George published in London in the 1730s.

Bishop Moore.

Orchard Street

The Namesake: one of the most beautiful orchards in the city, on the farm of James de Lancey.

The street was laid out through the orchard some time before 1767, but was not opened until 1806.

Orchard Street (looking south from Hester Street) in 1898, more than a century after it was laid out through James de Lancey's orchard.

Paladino Avenue

The Namesake: Anthony C. Paladino, member of a family described in city records as having been "early settlers" of the neighborhood who contributed greatly to its development.

The street's name was bestowed on it in 1954.

Overlook Terrace

The Namesake: its topographic characteristics.

A steeply rising street, the terrace at its highest point affords a view to the east that in the past must have been well worth looking at.

Park Avenue

The Namesake: inexplicable and nondescriptive when the name was bestowed.

Park Avenue began life as Fourth Avenue in the city plan of 1811, and promised even less than Fifth Avenue. A granite ridge ran its length and the planners deemed it impossible that it could ever become a real street. So when the city's first railroad, the New York & Harlem (see Prince Street) sought permission to extend its tracks above 14th Street and to use steam locomotives instead of horses, the city told it to take Fourth Avenue. The railroaders blasted out the granite and laid the tracks in a deep cut, which they crudely covered. But smoke from the engines belched through the ventilators in the cut, and Fourth Avenue attracted only the poorest of shack dwellers. (The Fourth Avenue Boys, a wicked gang, actually lived in the cut.) Eventually, the city made 42nd Street the southernmost limit for the use of steam locomotives — an edict that determined the location of Grand Central Terminal. But above 42nd Street the smoke continued to blight the area. Nevertheless, as early as 1860, Fourth Avenue from 34th to 36th streets was known as Park Avenue and by 1867 the name applied all the way to 42nd Street. On March 1, 1888, the Board of Aldermen resolved that "Fourth Avenue from 43rd to 96th Street hereafter be known as Park Avenue" and two weeks later the section from 96th Street to the Harlem was renamed. (The segment above the Harlem up to Fordham Road did not get the fancier name until 1896.) Once the railroad was electrified, early in this century, and the cut paved over, Park Avenue began to merit its name.

Park Avenue looking north from Grand Central Terminal.

Park Place and Park Row
The Namesake: City Hall Park, which was the common where cattle grazed before the present City Hall — the city's third — began to rise in 1803.

Park Row used to be Chatham Street, in honor of William Pitt the elder, Earl of Chatham. It was renamed in 1886; the area, close to City Hall, where the action was, had become to the then crowded and hotly competitive newspaper business what Seventh Avenue became to the garment industry. Park Place was Robinson Street until 1813. (Thomas Robinson was a prominent member of the Sons of Liberty in the pre-Revolutionary Era.)

New Yorkers reading about Dewey's victory in Manila Bay, as posted on the newspaper bulletin boards in Park Row, 1899.

Park Street
The Namesake: Columbus Park, which is bounded by Baxter, Bayard, Mulberry and Park streets.

The park occupies the site of a block of noisome tenements that were the targets of the crusading reformer Jacob Riis in the late 19th century. Riis' campaign impelled the city to wipe out the slum.

Park Terrace, East and West
The Namesake: nearby Isham Park.

Payson Avenue
The Namesake: the Reverend Dr. George S. Payson of Fort Washington Presbyterian Church.

Dr. Payson retired in 1920 after serving the church for 40 years.

Patchin Place
The Namesake: Aaron D. Patchin, son-in-law of Samuel Milligan (*see* Milligan Place).

Patchin met his future wife, Isabella Milligan, when Milligan engaged Patchin to survey newly acquired farmland in 1799. Theodore Dreiser lived in Patchin Place in 1895 when he was still a young journalist.

Theodore Dreiser in a photograph by Pirie MacDonald.

Pearl Street
The Namesake: mother-of-pearl, the oyster shells that virtually paved the street when it was the East River shore.

Before landfill left Pearl Street high and dry several blocks from the river, it was often called simply The Strand. The first city hall stood at 71–73 Pearl Street, a parking lot when this book went to press. The City Hall had begun life in 1641 as the Stadt-Herberg, or City Tavern: a five-story stone structure, it was built by Governor William Kieft, who had tired of entertaining visitors to New Amsterdam at home and needed an inn to which to send them. Twelve years later, the tavern became City Hall.

Peck Slip

The Namesake: Benjamin Peck, a pre-Revolutionary merchant who did business there.

The slip dates to 1755. In 1763, Peck constructed a brick market building to house what became known as Peck Slip Market.
Benjamin Peck, merchant.

Peretz Square

The Namesake: Isaac Loeb Peretz, author, essayist, poet and dramatist, who wrote in Hebrew and Yiddish and has been described as the father of modern Jewish literature.

Peretz was born in 1851 in Zamosc, Russian Poland. He practiced law in Zamosc for ten years and did not devote himself to writing until the Czarist government revoked his license as a lawyer on the ground that he was a radical: he thereupon moved to Warsaw, where he wrote in Yiddish, held various posts in the Jewish community and engaged in Socialist activity. Addressing himself to Socialists, he once wrote: "I hope for your victory, but I fear and dread it." When he died in 1915, 100,000 Warsaw Jews attended his funeral. The tiny New York square named for him, at East Houston Street and First Avenue, was dedicated on November 23, 1952 by the then Manhattan Borough President, Robert F. Wagner Jr., who said that Peretz's "writings gave hope and purpose to his people."

Perry Street

The Namesake: Commodore Oliver Hazard Perry, commander of the American fleet in the Battle of Lake Erie in the War of 1812.

Perry, who had fought Barbary pirates as well as the British, died of yellow fever in Trinidad when he was 34.

Commodore Oliver H. Perry at the Battle of Lake Erie.

Pershing Square

The Namesake: General John Joseph Pershing, commander of the American Expeditionary Force in Europe in World War I and the first General of the Armies since George Washington.

Humbly born in Missouri in 1860, Pershing taught school before winning admittance to West Point. Commissioned in the cavalry, he fought Apaches in Arizona in 1886, Sioux in Dakota in 1890, the Spanish in Cuba in 1898 and the Moros of Mindanao in the Philippines in 1903. For his service in the Philippines, President Theodore Roosevelt promoted him from captain to brigadier general, over the heads of 862 officers. He commanded the 1916 expedition into Mexico against Francisco Villa and at the entry of the United States into World War I in 1917 he was chosen to lead American troops in Europe. After the war, he served as chief of staff. He died in 1948 and is buried in Arlington.

General John Joseph Pershing

Pell Street

The Namesake: John Pell, like Joseph Mott of Mott Street, a prosperous butcher before the Revolution.

John Pell descended from John Pell, first lord of the Manor of Pelham, created in Governor Dongan's day (see Dongan Place). The Pells were long-time residents of what became Pell Street. One William Pell and Nicolas Mattyse applied to the Common Council in 1719 for permission to cut a street there but the project apparently was much delayed: Pell Street first appears on a 1776 map. Two years later, in 1778, Joshua Pell purchased twenty acres near The Bowery and Chatham Square from James de Lancey. But Joshua, a cousin of Sir Henry Clinton, was a Tory and his property was confiscated after the Revolution.

Peter Cooper Road

The Namesake: Cooper Village, the housing development abutting Stuyvesant Town.

Both the road and the houses commemorate Peter Cooper (see Cooper Square).

Pine Street

The Namesake: a little pine wood that had stood on the farm of Jan Jansen Damen, a leading burgher in the 1640s.

Pine Street did not get its name until after the Revolution: the street previously had been King Street. The city·fathers first considered changing the name of King Street to Congress Street but had second thoughts.

Pinehurst Avenue

The Namesake: Pinehurst, the estate of a man named C. P. Bucking.

Pitt Street

The Namesake: William Pitt, Earl of Chatham.

(See Chatham Square)

Pike Street, Pike Slip

The Namesake: Zebulon Montgomery Pike, soldier and explorer for whom Pikes Peak in Colorado also is named.

As a 26-year-old lieutenant in 1805, Pike led a party of 20 soldiers in exploring lands acquired in the Louisiana Purchase; the following year he was sent out again to treat with Indian tribes. In the War of 1812, promoted to inspector general, he commanded the campaign against Toronto, then called York. On April 27, 1813, as he and his troops were breaking into the town, retreating British forces set afire a store of ammunition; Pike was killed by a rock sent flying by the explosion.

Brigadier General Zebulon M. Pike.

Platt Street

The Namesake: Jacob S. Platt, a wealthy merchant of the 1800s.

Platt Street was laid out and named for Platt because in 1832 he acquired considerable property in the area.

Plaza Lafayette

The Namesake: Boulevard Lafayette, the name by which Broadway from 155th Street to 157th Street was known until 1899.

Riverside Drive from 158th Street to Dyckman Street also was known as the Boulevard Lafayette. That name was changed in 1905.

Pomander Walk

The Namesake: Pomander Walk in London and the stage play written around it.

The street and its houses were modeled on the English originals and on the stage set that simulated them. The play, *Pomander Walk,* opened on Broadway December 20, 1910, and ran for 143 performances, with an actress named Dorothy Parker in the leading role. The New York street was built in 1921.

Pleasant Avenue

The Namesake: its agreeable situation on the East River.

Pleasant Avenue was part of Avenue A when the city's grid plan was completed in 1811. But what is now Pleasant Avenue was separated from the rest of Avenue A by an East River bight and was given its own name in 1879. If its designation had not been changed then, it would be part of York Avenue and David Durk and Ira Silverman would have had to choose another title for their 1976 book about the narcotics racket, *The Pleasant Avenue Connection.*

Pleasant Avenue some decades ago.

Post Avenue

The Namesakes: The Post family, early settlers whose name originally was Postmael.

Hendrick Post, in 1737, married Jan Nagel's daughter Rebecca. (*See* Nagle Avenue.)

Prince Street

The Namesake: unidentified British royalty.

Prince Street was a terminus of New York's first railway, the New York & Harlem Railroad, which began operating along The Bowery between Prince Street and the future 14th Street on November 14, 1832. The cars were pulled by horses because the city feared—quite rightly—that locomotives would blow up. The railroad, later absorbed by the New York Central, was organized chiefly by Thomas Addis Emmet, physician, lawyer, New York State attorney general, Irish exile and brother of Robert Emmet, martyr of the fight for Irish independence. Thomas Emmet died in 1827 before the railroad became a reality.

Printing House Square

The Namesake: the newspaper, magazine, print-publishing and advertising firms that clustered there before the Civil War.

Among the organizations headquartered on the square were *The New York Times, Tribune, World, Scientific American* and Currier & Ives.

Reade Street

The Namesake: Joseph Reade, a warden of Trinity Church.

A Joseph Reade was a member of the governor's council in colonial days, but whether Trinity's Reade and the governor's Reade were one man is not clear. Reade Street appears on a 1797 map.

Rector Street
The Namesakes: the rectors of Trinity Church.

Successive rectors lived there. Before 1790, it was called Auchmuty Street, for the Reverend Dr. Samuel Auchmuty, but Rector was easier to pronounce.

The Rev. Samuel Auchmuty, D.D., Rector of Trinity Church.

Ridge Street
The Namesake: a ridge that topped a hill on the property of James de Lancey. (*See* Delancey Street.)

The street still slopes to the East River as the ridge did, but most of the hills and valleys were leveled by the city planners of 1807.

Riverview Terrace
The Namesake: its view of the East River.

The terrace is off Sutton Place.

Renwick Street
The Namesake: James Renwick, an English-born scientist who came here early in life and taught at Columbia for forty years.

Renwick was at the top of the class when he was graduated from Columbia in 1807. He died in 1863.

Columbia College, from which James Renwick was graduated in 1807.

Rivington Street
The Namesake: James Rivington, publisher of the pro-British newspaper *Royal Gazette* in New York during the Revolutionary War.

A successful bookseller and publisher in London, Rivington blew a fortune on horse races and high living and came to America in 1760 to start afresh. After establishing bookstores in Philadelphia, New York and Boston, Rivington founded a newspaper, *Rivington's New-York Gazetteer; or the Connecticut, New Jersey Hudson's River and Quebec Weekly Advertiser.* Because the paper printed both sides of every political issue, an unprecedented practice, its plant was wrecked by patriot extremists and put out of business. Under the British occupation of the city, Rivington resumed publication, and supported the King. Rivington Street was named for him during the war. The street name was retained and Rivington himself was allowed to stay after the British evacuation because he publicly repented his Tory sympathies and because, it was said, he had secretly aided Washington's spies in the city. But he did not continue his paper. An amiable, witty and intelligent man, Rivington died broke in New York on July 4, 1802.

Rivington's New-York Gazetteer for April 20, 1775; front-page news was Westchester's declaration of loyalty to George III.

Riverside Drive

The Namesake: the Hudson River, which it parallels, and Riverside Park. The Drive was originally known as Riverside Avenue.

As early as 1750, the bluffs overlooking the Hudson were becoming a fashionable suburb, with a few estates and mansions. The De Lancey family (*see* Delancey Street) had a house at what is now 86th Street and the Drive until 1777, when, one cold autumn night, American troops burned it down because of the De Lanceys' Tory sympathies. (The women of the family fled in their nightgowns and one of them took shelter in a dog kennel.) Construc-tion of Riverside Park was proposed in 1865 in a pamphlet by William R. Martin and a law authorizing it was passed in Albany in 1867. (Before Home Rule, cities in New York State were beholden to the legislature for everything.) William Marcy Tweed, then commissioner of public works, was among the earliest to buy lots nearby, and the area became a prized neighborhood. Land for the park was acquired in 1872, at a cost of $6,174,120.80. Frederick Law Olmsted, the creator of Central Park and Prospect Park, designed Riverside Park by March 29, 1873. The park was completed as far north as 129th Street by 1885 and ten years later *The New York Times* editorialized: "There is no boulevard in all the world that competes with Riverside Drive in natural beauty." The park was extended by stages, with the purchases of additional land in 1891, 1899, 1900, 1901 and 1902 and the drive grew with the park, incorporating an already existing boulevard above 155th Street.

Bicycling by moonlight along the Drive.

Robert F. Wagner Sr. Place

The Namesake: Senator Robert F. Wagner, author of the Wagner Labor Relations Act that stimulated the unionization of workers during President Franklin D. Roosevelt's New Deal.

German-born and an 1898 graduate of CCNY, Wagner was elected to the state legislature in 1905 and subsequently served as lieutenant-governor and State Supreme Court justice before going to Washington. He was a U.S. senator from 1927 to 1949, when he resigned. He died in 1953.

Senator Robert F. Wagner, Sr.

Rockefeller Plaza

The Namesake: Rockefeller Center, built in the 1930s economic depression largely on land leased from Columbia University by the Rockefeller family.

The center embodies the site of Elgin Garden, New York's first botanical garden. Dr. David Hosack, the physician who attended the dying Alexander Hamilton after his duel with Aaron Burr, established the garden in 1801, having paid $4,807.36 for 256 lots, plus an annual rent of 16 bushels of wheat. But the garden was too far out of town to attract many visitors and Hosack could not afford the rising taxes, so he turned the property over to the state in 1814. The state bestowed it on Columbia University in compensation for vast acreage that Columbia ceded to New Hampshire in the settlement of a New York–New Hampshire boundary dispute.

John D. Rockefeller.

Rose Street

The Namesake: probably Captain Joseph Rose, a distiller and merchant, who died in 1807, age 72, and was buried in Trinity Churchyard.

Joseph Rose, listed in the City Directory for 1786, lived at 135 Water Street; a J. Rose, a hairdresser, resided at 141 Water Street. The name of Rose Street dates to 1794. Rose Street in the first half of the 19th century was a blue-collar residential neighborhood. One so-called mechanic who lived there was James Harper (1795–1869), a master printer who founded Harper & Bros., now Harper and Row. Harper gave Rose Street a few years of fame and glory: he was elected mayor in 1844 of "the most prosperous and worst governed city in the world" and during his reform administration his home at No. 50 Rose Street was the mayor's official residence, distinguished by the lamps that flanked the doorway.

James Harper (1795-1869).

Roosevelt Square

The Namesake: Theodore
Roosevelt, the 26th President.

The square was named for "Teddy"
in 1919, the year he died.

*Theodore Roosevelt and the Rough Riders at
the Battle of San Juan Hill in 1898.*

Rutgers Street, Rutgers Slip
The Namesake: Henry Rutgers, wealthy Revolutionary War patriot, legislator and Tammany bigwig.

Member of the Class of 1766 at King's College (now Columbia), Rutgers was a descendant of Rutger Jacobsen van Schoenderwoert, who arrived in 1636 and grew rich as a brewer, merchant and Manhattan landowner. Henry was the son of Hendrick Rutgers and the former Catherine de Peyster. Before the Revolution, Henry convened meetings of the Sons of Liberty on his farm and later fought as a captain in the American army at the Battle of White Plains. After the war he served as an assemblyman and raised money for Tammany's first Wigwam. New Jersey's Queens College was renamed for him at the urging of his friend Philip Milledolor, the college's president, who hoped for a big bequest to the institution. Rutgers left $200 for a bell and $5,000 as an endowment.

St. James Place
The Namesake: St. James Roman Catholic Church at 23 Oliver Street.

Alfred E. Smith, the governor of New York who was the Democratic candidate for President in 1928, was a parishioner of the church; the street, formerly called New Bowery, was renamed in 1947 in tribute to him, The street is the location of the oldest surviving mark of the white man on Manhattan—the graveyard of *Shearith Israel* (Remnant of Israel), the Spanish and Portuguese synagogue. The tiny cemetery was established in 1683 and was the synagogue's second: the first, probably just above Wall Street, long since has vanished. The plot is the resting place of Gershom Mendes Seixas, rabbi of the synagogue for fifty years, from 1766 to 1816, and trustee of Columbia College. A Revolutionary patriot, Seixas was one of fourteen clergymen to officiate at President Washington's inauguration. His sermons were so highly regarded that he was invited to preach in St. Paul's Chapel and one of them, for Thanksgiving, was published as a pamphlet which the *Daily Gazette* for December 23, 1789, commended to the attention "of every pious reader, whether Jew or Christian."

Stone in the graveyard of Shearith Israel synagogue, St. James Place.

Rutherford Place
The Namesake: Colonel John Rutherford, a member of the committee that laid out Manhattan's streets and avenues beginning in 1807.

Ryder's Alley
The Namesake: undetermined.

Before 1842, it was known as Eden's Alley.

St. Clair Place
The Namesake: St. Clair Pollock, the child buried in the solitary grave in Riverside Park near Grant's Tomb.

St. Clair, whose gravestone reads "To the memory of an amiable child" who "died 15th July, 1797, in the fifth year of his age," was the son of Carlisle Pollock, for whom Carlisle Street is named (*see* Carlisle Street). St. Clair drowned in the Hudson while fishing with his father from Fishing Rock, at the foot of their country property. The boy's first name honored family friends named Sinclair.

St. Johns Lane

The Namesake: St. John's Chapel, which stood there.

Garden of St. John's Episcopalian Chapel in the 1930s.

St. Lukes Place

The Namesake: St. Luke's Chapel (of Trinity Parish).

St. Marks Place

The Namesake: Church of St. Mark's in-the-Bouwerie.

The church was built between 1795 and 1799 and stands on the site of Peter Stuyvesant's Bouwerie Chapel.

St. Vartan's Park

The Namesake: St. Vartan's Armenian National Cathedral, across the street from the park.

The tiny park between First and Second Avenues and East 35th and East 36th streets used to be called St. Gabriel's Park, for St. Gabriel's Church. But St. Gabriel's was demolished to make way for the Queens-Midtown Tunnel and the park acquired its present name in May 1978.

St. Nicholas Avenue

The Namesake: New Amsterdam's patron saint, in a belated gesture. New Amsterdam's first real church, built in 1642, was called the Church of St. Nicholas because the saint was the figurehead of *New Netherland,* the ship that brought the first colonists.

Named in 1901, St. Nicholas Avenue had been Kings Way, Great Post Road, Albany Post Road, Queens Road and Kingsbridge Road. It originated, it appears, as an Indian trail which became the road from the town of Harlem to the ferry established at Spuyten Duyvil in 1669.

Harlem's freeholders undertook in 1676 "to make the road" to the crossing. The renaming of St. Nicholas Avenue took place about the time—give or take ten years—that Amsterdam, Columbus and other avenues were given their present designations to make them more attractive socially. But way back in 1866, the Central Park commissioners had been instructed by the state legislature to lay out "Avenue St. Nicholas and Manhattan Street" to make Central Park more accessible.

The St. Nicholas Lagerbier House and Restaurant, St. Nicholas Avenue, at the turn of the century.

St. Nicholas Terrace

The Namesake: St. Nicholas Park, which the terrace borders.

The terrace was named in 1891, presumably in anticipation of the park's construction. St. Nicholas Avenue did not get its present name until ten years later.

Samuel Marx Triangle

The Namesake: Sam Marx, who died a few weeks after his election to Congress in 1922.

An auctioneer by profession, Sam Marx had served two terms as alderman before winning a congressional seat and was the Democratic leader of the 17th Assembly District.

Schiff Parkway

The Namesake: Jacob Schiff, financier and philanthropist.

Schiff came to New York from Frankfort, Germany, in 1865, at age 18 and amassed a fortune. Schiff Parkway was part of Delancey Street until the approaches to the Williamsburg Bridge were redesigned.

Sara Roosevelt Parkway

The Namesake: Sara Delano (Mrs. James) Roosevelt, mother of President Franklin D. Roosevelt.

A handsome, wealthy aristocrat, Mrs. Roosevelt counted among her ancestors at least two members of the Pilgrim colony at Plymouth. One was Philippe de la Noye, a Huguenot who came to America in 1621 to continue his wooing of Priscilla Mullens, whom he lost to John ("Why don't you speak for yourself, John?") Alden. The other was Isaac Allerton, who arrived on the Mayflower in 1620 and served Plymouth Colony as business agent for ten years, until he was suspected of fraud and left. (He prospered in New Amsterdam, where he settled.) Though impeccably WASP, Mrs. Roosevelt had the qualities of the legendary Jewish mother. She was widowed when Franklin, her only son, was 18 and until she died at 86—on September 8, 1941— her life centered on her offspring. Franklin returned her devotion, but Eleanor Roosevelt, his wife, did not consider her the ideal mother-in-law.

Sara Delano Roosevelt, mother of the 31st President.

Scott Square

The Namesake: John Morin Scott, a busy and prosperous New York City lawyer, pre-Revolutionary agitator, Revolutionary War general and frequent holder of public office.

Great grandson of Sir John Scott, a Scottish baronet, grandson of a settler who came to America in 1700 and son of a New York City merchant and his Huguenot wife, Scott was born in New York in 1730, and was graduated from Yale in 1746. He served as an alderman from 1756 to 1761, and then became one of the organizers of the Sons of Liberty. (Even critics of British rule considered Scott an extremist.) When New York organized itself as a state rather than a colony, Scott was elected to the new State Supreme Court, but he refused to take his place on the bench because John Jay beat him out for the chief justiceship (*see* Jay Street). In 1777, Scott ran unsuccessfully for the governorship against George Clinton and Philip Schuyler. The following year he was appointed New York's Secretary of State. He found time also to fight in the Battle of Long Island as a brigadier general, to serve in the state senate from 1777 to 1782, and to sit in the Continental Congress from 1779 to 1783. As an attorney, he won the praise of John Adams. An exile from the city during the British occupation in wartime, Scott returned to his handsome rural residence in what is now West 43rd Street, between Eighth and Ninth avenues, as soon as the British left in 1783. But he died in 1784 of acute rheumatism that had been aggravated by exposure while he was a soldier.

Seaman Avenue

The Namesake: Henry B. Seaman, member of a prominent family that lived north of the Isham tract (*see* Isham Street and Isham Park), when the street was opened in 1908.

Of ancient English lineage, the Seamans in this country date back to Captain John Seaman, who arrived in America in 1630 and by 1653 owned 12,000 acres in the vicinity of Hempstead, Long Island. Among Captain John's descendants was Dr. Valentine Seaman, who with several colleagues introduced vaccination against smallpox to the United States in the early 1800s. Dr. Seaman's son John bought 25 acres between 214th and 217th streets and between Kingsbridge Road and Spuyten Duyvil Creek, and John's brother Valentine built a house atop a hill between what are now Park Terrace East and Park Terrace West.

Sherman Avenue

The Namesakes: the Sherman family, working-class folk who for more than a century, beginning in 1807, made their home on a little waterway that became known as Shermans Creek. About 1815, they occupied a fisherman's shack below Fort George Hill.

The street traverses the land once owned by Dyckmans. Shermans Creek, a deep indentation in the Harlem River's bank, originally was called the Half-Kill, to distinguish it from the Great Kill, i.e. the Harlem River. The creek constituted an important landmark in colonial days.

Sherman Square

The Namesake: General William Tecumseh Sherman, the Civil War general best known for his march through Georgia and his capture of Atlanta.

A West Pointer who fought the Seminole Indians in Florida and the Mexicans in California before the Civil War, Sherman was a businessman and a lawyer when not serving in the army: his New York home was in the vicinity of Sherman Square, and he died there in 1891. The equestrian statue of him erected in 1903 was executed by Augustus St. Gaudens.

William Tecumseh Sherman, Civil War General.

Sheridan Square

The Namesake: Philip Henry Sheridan, the Union's most brilliant cavalry commander in the Civil War.

The Albany-born son of recent Irish immigrants, Sheridan was short and fat and an unlikely-looking West Pointer, but, a lieutenant at the Civil War's start, he was a major general by 1864. He became a full general shortly before he died in 1888 and Sheridan Square was named for him in 1896.

Philip Henry Sheridan, commanding the Department of the Missouri in 1868.

Sickles Street

The Namesake: the Sickles family, which owned a tract between Broadway and the Hudson from 199th Street to 201st Street.

The first Sickles in New Netherlands (who spelled it Sickels) was Zacharias, a venturesome Viennese who was in Curaçao when Peter Stuyvesant visited that island in 1655. Zacharias accompanied Stuyvesant to New Amsterdam but settled first in Fort Orange (Albany), where he was *rattel watch* (night watchman), town crier, keeper of the city gates and town herdsman. He moved to the city in 1693 after some of his sons had preceded him.

South William Street

The Namesake: its location below William Street, which immortalizes William Beeckman.

South William Street has had many names: it first was called *Slyck Steegh*, for "muddy lane"; in 1657 it became Glaziers Street because Evert Duyckingh, a glazier, lived there; then it was Mill Street, for a succession of mills situated there since 1628. It was known also as Jews Alley and Synagogue Alley because of the Jewish house of worship in the street. It acquired its present name in 1738.

Millstones remaining from the 17th century, on the site of the first grist mill in New Amsterdam —a muddy lane at first, later South William Street.

Sniffen Court

The Namesake: John Sniffen, a builder listed in the 1859–1860 New York City Directory as having offices at 206 Eldridge Street and as living at 152 Henry Street. On behalf of four real estate men who owned four lots on the site of the court, Sniffen erected ten stables and coach houses for the use of Murray Hill gentry.

The court is a tiny enclave on the south side of East 36th Street near Third Avenue. The original structures were remodeled into dwellings in the 1920s, when automobiles had replaced horse-drawn carriages. The wall at the far end of the court enclosed the studio of Malvina Hoffman, the sculptress. The mews was designated a historic landmark in 1966.

Sniffen Court, more than a century after it was built.

South Street

The Namesake: something of a misnomer: though the street's lower end is close to Manhattan's southern tip, South Street might better have been called East Street since it parallels the East River.

Built on landfill at the end of the 17th century, South Street thrived through the 19th century as the center of the city's sea commerce: tall-masted ships crowded its docks and the river. In the great fire of 1835 that devastated much of lower Manhattan, 76 of South Street's buildings were consumed. Some of the street's past is preserved or re-created in the South Street Seaport Museum.

South Street in 1878, showing the bows of docked sailing ships, the signs of sail makers, manufacturers of nautical instruments, and others, and —in the distance —the first cables being strung for Brooklyn Bridge.

Spring Street

The Namesake: a spring that originated there, at West Broadway, and once served as a source of water for residents. The street, formerly called Brannon Street because a man of that name had a garden at the spot, crossed Richmond Hill, the glamorous estate owned by Aaron Burr.

The spring, though imprisoned underground, still flows: it flooded a basement in West Broadway early in 1974. And it may be the haunt of one of the city's few reported ghosts—that of a girl named Juliana Elmore Sands, who was found dead in the Spring Street Well at Broadway at New Year's, 1800. Her sweetheart, Levi Weeks, was charged with her murder but defense counsel Alexander Hamilton and Aaron Burr won his acquittal. For years after Juliana's death, newspapers recounted stories of her ghost having been sighted at the scene: in 1974 a resident of 535 Broadway, at Spring Street, claimed he had been visited by a female apparition with long grey hair who was clad in a robe of moss and seaweed. The apparition had emerged, he said, from his waterbed.

Staff Street

The Namesake: a neighborhood boy killed fighting in World War I.

Like Henshaw Street, Staff Street was named at the instance of Inwood Post, American Legion, but the post's early records have been lost and nothing more is known of poor Staff.

Stanton Street

The Namesake: a foreman on the estate of the De Lancey family.

The street was opened in 1806, but what Stanton did to merit the honor, and even his first name, are unrecorded.

Staple Street

The Namesake: staple products that were unloaded there.

Under Dutch law that was effective in New Netherland, ships in transit had to pay duty on their cargo or offer the cargo for sale. In New Amsterdam, Staple Street was the marketplace for such goods.

Bartering for staples on the docks of New York in colonial days.

Spruce Street

The Namesake: undetermined.

The name was changed from George Street in 1817.

A variety of the coniferous, evergreen spruce tree, Picea excelsa.

State Street

The Namesake: New York State, for which it was named by the Common Council in 1795.

Before its rebaptism, State Street was called Copsey Street, for the Indian village of Kopsee that had existed nearby. At the time of its change of name, the street was one of the city's most elegant residential areas and it remained fashionable until after the Civil War.

Stone Street

The Namesake: cobblestones that made it the city's first paved street in 1658.

Originally it was Brouwer (Brewer) Street because Oloff Stevensen van Cortlandt, the first of the Van Cortlandts in New York, had a brewery there. But the brewery horses raised so much dust and dirtied so many curtains that Mrs. Van Cortlandt and her neighbors demanded that the city pave the street. Only three years later, the job was completed: the residents paid the costs.

Stuyvesant Alley, Stuyvesant Oval and Stuyvesant Place

The Namesake: Stuyvesant Town, the housing complex which gets its name from Stuyvesant Square nearby (see following entry).

Stuyvesant Square

The Namesake: Peter G. Stuyvesant, a 19th century descendant of the early governor.

Peter G. Stuyvesant and his wife donated the land for the square to the city in 1836.

Pear tree planted by Governor Stuyvesant survived into the 19th century. It stood at the northeast corner of Third Avenue and 13th Street.

Straus Park

The Namesake: Isidor Straus, who with his brother Nathan built R.H. Macy & Co. into the world's largest retail store.

German-born, Straus grew up in Georgia and served the Confederacy on a purchasing mission in England before settling in New York in 1865. He and his father took over Macy's crockery and glassware department in 1874; by 1896 he and Nathan owned the store. Active in politics, he campaigned for his friend President Grover Cleveland in 1892, influenced Cleveland's monetary policies, and was himself elected to Congress. He refused to run for a second term and twice turned down the Democratic nomination for mayor of New York, in 1901 and 1909. His philanthropies included the East Side's Educational Alliance, of which he was president from its founding in 1893 until his death. He and his wife Ida went down with the *Titanic* in 1912: she refused to enter a lifeboat without him and, despite urging, he would not take a place in one until all the women and children had been accommodated.

Fountain in Straus Park, commemorating Isidore and Ida Straus, who died at sea in 1912.

Sutton Place and Sutton Square

The Namesake: Effingham B. Sutton, 19th-century dry goods merchant who foresaw a great future for the east end of 57th Street as a residential area and in 1875 organized a syndicate to promote the neighborhood.

Sutton made his money out of the 1849 California gold rush. When news of gold's discovery reached New York, Sutton dispatched the fastest available ship with picks, shovels, tents and flour, and the vessel returned seven months later laden with nuggets. Sutton added ships and started the first clipper service to San Francisco. His real estate venture proved less successful: his vision was good but his timing was bad and the East Side boom was long delayed. Sutton Place became fashionable only when Anne Morgan of the Morgan banking family moved there in 1921.

A prospector around 1860, whose pose with a bag of "gold" is a claim that he had done what merchants such as Effingham Sutton actually achieved: made a fortune from the Gold Rush that began in 1849.

Suffolk Street
The Namesake: the English county of that name.

Sylvan Court, Place and Terrace
The Namesake: somebody's fancy.

Szold Place
The Namesake: Henrietta Szold, founder of Hadassah, the women's Zionist organization, and its president from 1912 to 1926.

Miss Szold was frequently described as the "most brilliant Jewish woman in America."

Miss Henrietta Szold, president of Hadassah from 1912-1926 (with one year's rest in 1922).

Sullivan Street
The Namesake: Brigadier General John Sullivan, one of the ablest of the Revolutionary War commanders.

A New Hampshire lawyer, Sullivan was a member of the first Continental Congress. As a soldier, he fought in the battles of Long Island, Trenton, Brandywine and Germantown, among others; but he is best remembered for a punitive expedition he led against the Indians of the Six Nations who had ravaged Western New York. His retaliatory methods provoked wide criticism but Congress commended him, after which he quit the army. From 1789 until he died in 1795, he served as a federal judge.

Taras Shevchenko Place

The Namesake: the 19th Century Ukrainian writer, artist and political activist.

Until May 1978, the tiny thoroughfare between East Sixth and East Seventh streets was called Hall Place, in memory of an otherwise forgotten man from whom the city bought the land for the street in 1830.

Teunissen Place

The Namesake: Tobias Teunissen, an early settler in upper Manhattan who was killed by Indians.

A wool washer by trade and a night watchman at the University of Leyden, Teunissen sailed for America in 1636 after losing his entire family. He worked three years as a farmhand for Dr. Jean Mousnier de la Montagne, a former Leyden medical student who was New Amsterdam's first doctor, then set up his own farm. Remarried, and a leading citizen, he prospered until 64 canoe-loads of Indians descended on Manhattan in a three-day raid that began September 15, 1655. Teunissen was one of fifty whites killed; his wife, his small son and his three stepchildren were carried off into captivity.

Thames Street

The Namesake: debatable.

Nicholas Bayard deeded the land to the city in 1690 and it was called Little Stone Street until 1766. Whether its present name is for London's River Thames or is a corruption of Thomas is not known.

Thayer Street

The namesake: Francis Thayer, an attorney active in improving the area.

The street was named for Thayer in 1911. It had previously been called Union Place.

Theatre Alley

The Namesake: the Park Theatre, the city's second, which opened January 29, 1798, with a performance of *As You Like It*.

The theater's stage door entrance was on the narrow passageway just east of Park Row. Carriages taking theater-goers to the stage door entered the alley from Ann Street, at one end, or from Beekman Street at the other, causing monumental traffic jams, until the alley was made a one-way street – the city's first. The theater was designed by the French refugee brothers, Joseph Francis and Charles Mangin (*see* Mangin Street).

Lithograph of Park Theatre and part of Park Row in 1831.

Thompson Street

The Namesake: William Thompson, an Irish-born Pennsylvanian who was a brigadier general in the Revolutionary War.

Thompson led a corps of giant sharpshooters from Pennsylvania to the defense of Boston after the Battle of Bunker Hill and was officially thanked by General Washington for repelling a British attack. Later, he commanded a detachment of 2,000 men in the 1776 invasion of Canada, but a guide treacherously headed him into a swamp where he was captured. Paroled, he complained to Congress that Thomas McKean, a congressman, had hindered his release and Congress found Thompson guilty "of an insult to the honor and dignity of this house." Thompson died back home in Pennsylvania a month before Lord Cornwallis surrendered at Yorktown, ending the conflict.

Thomas Street

The Namesake: Thomas Lispenard, son of Anthony Lispenard.

(*See* Leonard Street and Lispenard Street.)

Tiemann Place

The Namesake: Mayor Daniel F. Tiemann, elected in 1858.

A paint and dye manufacturer, Tiemann had a tree-shaded home on the north side of 127th Street between Broadway and the Hudson. His paint and dye plant stood north of his house. As mayor, he ordered the placing of street names on streetlight poles.

Daniel F. Tiemann, Mayor of New York. Engraving from a photograph made in Mathew Brady's studio.

Times Square

The Namesake: the Times Building which Adolph Ochs erected in 1904 when he moved *The New York Times* there from Park Row. The building subsequently was known as the Times Tower and, after remodeling, as the Allied Chemical Building and No. 1 Times Square, its current name.

Formerly Longacre Square, Times Square was renamed on April 13, 1904, at the instance of August Belmont, whose Interborough Rapid Transit Company was constructing the subway. He wrote to Alexander E. Orr, president of the Board of Rapid Transit Commissioners: "No station on our route is liable to be more active or important than that at 42nd Street and Broadway. We are planning, in connection with the Times Building, to have access to it from Seventh Avenue. Owing to the conspicuous position which the *Times* holds, it being one of the leading New York journals, it would seem fitting that the square on which the building stands should be known as Times Square and the station named Times Square Station." The *Times* moved its presses into the building on December 31, 1904, to the accompaniment of a great show of fireworks that started the tradition of New Year's Eve celebrations in Times Square. *The New York Times* within a few years left the square for West 43rd. Street but nobody would dare to change the square's world-famous name.

The newly-built Times Tower in Times Square.

Tompkins Square

The Namesake: Daniel D. Tompkins, four-term governor of New York State, Vice President of the U.S., and a military commander in the War of 1812.

Tompkins initiated the 1817 law that abolished slavery in New York State on July 4, 1827. He fought for decent treatment of blacks and Indians. He urged improvements in the school system and he sought to liberalize the criminal code. He demanded that the well-off as well as the poor serve in the militia for the defense of the state. He opposed the rapid proliferation of banks which, in those days, did not guarantee a friend behind every desk. In short, Tompkins rode at the head of the good guys—and he found the going rough. Born in Scarsdale in 1774, the son of a Revolutionary patriot, he began practicing law and politics soon after his graduation from Columbia in 1795. By 1803 he was elected to the Assembly, and the following year to Congress. He resigned as Congressman to become a state Supreme Court justice, and in 1807 he defeated the incumbent Morgan Lewis for the governorship. He was re-elected in 1810, 1813 and 1816. The troubles that were to make him a tragic figure began during his governorship, with the War of 1812. As governor, Tompkins was a commander-in-chief of the militia which was to defend New York. Not only did he lack funds and an adequate staff, but also, he had a rag-tag, disgruntled soldiery because his own Assembly, dominated by the upper classes, refused until 1814 to reform the unfair militia system. In the war's darkest days, when New York was paralyzed by fear of imminent British attack, he was handed command of a military district embracing southern New York and eastern New Jersey. He managed to round up 25,000 troops for the defense of New York City. But *snafu* is no modern military invention. Tompkins had to pay the troops himself —borrowing the money, some of it on his own signature. It also fell upon him to meet the costs of the Military Academy at West Point and of the defense of New England. In the confusion, he neglected to keep careful books—and he wound up at the war's end in heavy debt, technically, to both the state and the federal government. It took years for Albany and Washington to wipe the slate clean: in the meantime, his supposed debts became a political issue and a weapon of mud-slingers. Though he was elected Vice President of the U.S. in 1817 and re-elected in 1821, his problems cost him election as governor in 1820. Broken in spirit, exhausted by overwork and drinking heavily, he died in 1825 at his Staten Island home. He was 51 years old.

Tudor City Place

The Namesake: Tudor City, the midtown apartment complex.

The name was changed from Prospect Place in 1948.

Trinity Place

The Namesake: Trinity Church.

Trinity Place, which runs behind the church, was variously known until 1843 as Lumber Street and Lombard Street. The present name was bestowed that year.

Trimble Place

The Namesake: George Trimble, 19th-century merchant, a director of New York Hospital and an officer of the Public School Society.

Trimble died in 1872 and was honored with surprising alacrity on the part of the city fathers: Trimble Place appears in a city directory for 1874.

George Trimble, officer of the Public School Society.

Union Square

The Namesake: the junction of many streets and roads there.

The square was named Union Place in 1808, when the commissioners who were laying out the city on the grid plan decreed that the area should remain open. It was renamed Union Square in 1832.

Bird's-eye view of Union Square, looking south.

United Nations Plaza

The Namesake: The United Nations, whose headquarters towers over the plaza. The General Assembly building, the headquarters' first in the complex, opened in 1952.

The plaza extends from 42nd to 48th streets and from First Avenue to the Franklin D. Roosevelt Drive and covers the scene of a famous murder in Dutch days. In 1626, years before the murder, three white men who worked for Peter Minuit mugged two Weekquaeskeek Indian braves and the 12-year-old nephew of one of them near what is now Foley Square. The Indians had walked down from the neighborhood of Irvington-on-Hudson laden with beaver skins. The muggers killed the uncle. The other man and the nephew got away. And one summer day in 1641, the nephew, who had waited 15 years for revenge on whites, strode into the isolated house of Claes Smits on the East River at what is now 45th Street, offered to trade beaverskins for duffel cloth, and clobbered Smits with an ax when Smits bent down to reach for the cloth. Poor Smits had had nothing to do with the 1626 mugging, but to the Indian one white was as bad as another. Governor Willem Kieft sent a posse of 80 men after the nephew but the posse got lost and the nephew never was captured. The 1626 killers too went unpunished because the authorities never learned of their crime until Smits was murdered.

The United Nations, framed by the towers of the Empire State (left) and Chrysler buildings (right).

University Place

The Namesake: New York University's campus.

Formerly part of Wooster Street, University Place was given its present name in 1838, a year after New York University erected its first building on Washington Square.

Vandam Street

The Namesake: Anthony Van Dam, an early 19th Century alderman.

The name Van Dam had long been familiar to New Yorkers when the city bestowed it on the street in 1807. It had been made so by Rip Van Dam, a feisty Albany-born Dutchman who never mastered English but who governed the British province of New York from August 1, 1731 to August 1, 1732 — the period between the death of one British governor and the arrival of another. A prosperous merchant, Rip Van Dam spent most of his life in political battles. He bitterly fought Jacob Leisler, the popularly chosen governor who was unjustly hanged in 1691; more than forty years later he fought just as bitterly against William Cosby, his own successor as governor. When Cosby sued him and won, Van Dam simply ignored the court's ruling and kept the money involved. In another battle with Cosby, Rip Van Dam backed John Peter Zenger, the newspaper editor whom Cosby had imprisoned, and whose acquittal on charges of libel established the freedom of the press in America. Rip Van Dam's birthdate is unknown, but he married in 1684 and died in 1749.

above: The Vanderbilt mansion on Fifth Avenue, 1895.

below: Cornelius Vanderbilt. who became the nation's most conspicuous millionaire after the death of John Jacob Astor.

Vanderbilt Avenue

The Namesakes: the Vanderbilt family which long controlled the New York Central Railroad.

The Vanderbilt fortune was founded by Cornelius, who bought a sailboat about 1810, when he was 16, to ferry passengers and farm produce between his native Staten Island and Manhattan. From that beginning, he built a fleet of coastal and trans-Atlantic steamships that earned him the honorary title of "Commodore"; but late in life he switched to railroading. His merger of the New York Central, which ran from Albany to Buffalo, and the Hudson River Road from New York City to Albany provided the backbone for what became the gigantic New York Central. He was succeeded in control of the railroad by his son William Henry and then by William Henry's eldest son Cornelius.

Varick Street

The Namesake: Colonel Richard Varick, Revolutionary patriot and mayor of New York from 1789 to 1801. He owned the land through which the street was cut. (Another mayor, Fiorello H. LaGuardia, was born in a tenement at No. 7 Varick Street in 1882, when most of the neighbors were black or Irish).

Aide to Benedict Arnold at West Point, Varick fell under suspicion when Arnold defected. But a court of inquiry that Varick himself demanded acquitted him with honor. Suspicion persisted, though, and General Washington showed his confidence in Varick by appointing him to organize all Continental Army records. After the war and before becoming mayor, Varick served as the city recorder, as Speaker of the Assembly and as Attorney General. With Samuel Jones (of Great Jones Street) he codified New York State's laws. He married Isaac Roosevelt's daughter Maria but they had no children.

Vermilyea Avenue

The Namesake: The family of Isaac Vermeille, who settled in upper Manhattan in 1663 with his wife and four children.

Isaac Vermeille, a Walloon, was born in London, where his parents were refugees; in this country, Vermeille became a constable and a magistrate. His descendants spell the name Vermilye as well as Vermilyea.

Vestry Street

The Namesake: the nearby vestry house of St. John's Chapel.

The land for the street was ceded by Trinity Church.

Vesey Street

The Namesake: the Reverend William Vesey, first rector of Trinity Church, which he served from Christmas Day, 1697, until his death in 1746.

A Harvard graduate (Class of 1693), Vesey was the son of a Massachusetts farmer pilloried for "desperate words" against the king. To qualify for Trinity's pulpit, Vesey had to be ordained in the Church of England and Trinity's wardens and vestrymen lent him £95 to go to London. As rector, Vesey was in frequent conflict with British governors who disagreed with his broad claims for the church's rights and prerogatives. In his less combative moments, Vesey administered charities and established a free school which took in blacks. When he died he had charge of 22 congregations.

Wadsworth Avenue

The Namesake: James Samuel Wadsworth, wealthy anti-slavery upstater without military training who distinguished himself as a Union general in the Civil War. He was the Republican candidate for governor of New York in 1862 while serving in the army.

In his fifties, father of six children and seemingly unsuited in every way for soldiering, Wadsworth went to the front at the war's outbreak and won a reluctantly granted appointment as aide to General Irvin McDowell. He rode so hard and served so efficiently at the Battle of Bull Run that he promptly was commissioned a brigadier general. Wadsworth's division held off Confederate forces for three days at Gettysburg, despite grave losses. Wadsworth himself was killed at Chancellorsville after two horses had been shot from under him and a third, uncontrollable in its terror, had carried him to the Confederate lines.

Brigadier General J. S. Wadsworth, third from the right, and his staff.

Wall Street

The Namesake: a wall erected in 1653 to defend the city against an expected attack from New England: Britain and The Netherlands were at war at the time. New Amsterdam's Dutch called it *De Waal*.

Erection of the wall became a project involving all male residents, after bids by private contractors were deemed too high. The city fathers directed that "citizens without exception" should begin immediately "digging a ditch from the East River to the North River, 4 to 5 feet deep and 11 to 12 feet wide at the top, sloping a little towards the bottom"; that the carpenters should "be urged to prepare jointly the stakes and rails"; that "the soldiers and other servants of the company, with the free negroes, no one excepted," should "complete the work on the Fort by making a parapet and the farmers be summoned to haul pieces of turf," that the sawyers should "immediately begin to saw planks of four inches thickness for gun carriages and platforms." The wall had one entrance, at Wall and Pearl streets, known as the Watergate. The attack did not come until 1664, by sea, and the wall never served its purpose. The British demolished it in 1699.

The financial district in the early 1900s. Camera was aimed north on Broad Street towards Wall Street.

Walker Street

The Namesake: Benjamin Walker, Revolutionary War soldier and one-term representative to Congress from New York.

A youthful English immigrant who had set up as a New York merchant, Walker became a captain in the 2nd New York Regiment at the outbreak of the Revolution and subsequently served on the staffs of "Baron" F. W. A. H. F. von Steuben and General Washington. After the war, he became secretary to the governor of New York, then entered the brokerage business. He served in Congress 1801-1803.

Warren Street

The Namesake: Admiral Sir Peter Warren, who acquired 300 acres in Greenwich Village in 1744, paying with part of the treasure he had captured from 24 enemy French and Spanish ships—one single prize carried plate worth £250,000.

A charmer who was New York's earliest social lion, Warren had a palatial house in the block bounded by Charles, Perry, Bleecker and Tenth streets. He married the fetching Susannah de Lancey, whose father, Oliver, headed the firm that served as Warren's agent in selling his loot. After his return to Britain, Warren became an MP: he is buried in Westminster Abbey. Long after his death, his estate—which had been divided among his three daughters—was cut up by the city plan of 1811 into 12- and 15-acre plots for small farms and country seats. But his house survived until 1865, when it was replaced by brick residences.

Wanamaker Place

The Namesake: John Wanamaker, dynamic, innovative Philadelphian who founded the Wanamaker department stores: his main New York store stood on what is now Wanamaker Place.

One of seven children born on Philadelphia's outskirts, Wanamaker began working at age 13 as a $1.50-a-week errand boy, then became a salesman of men's clothing. Religious and a prohibitionist, he temporarily abandoned retailing at age 19 to take a $1,000-a-year post as a YMCA secretary, the organization's first to receive pay. Four years later, he and a brother-in-law started a men's clothing store in Philadelphia that within a decade was the nation's biggest: Wanamaker offered money-back guarantees and advertised and promoted vigorously. In one vast promotion at the time of the Centennial Exposition in 1876, he took over a Pennsylvania Railroad freight depot and turned it into a department store that drew droves of Exposition visitors. He acquired his first New York store in 1896 by buying the old A.T. Stewart shop from its receivers. An active Republican, he was appointed postmaster-general in 1889 and began advocating government ownership of telephones and telegraphs. He was still actively working when he died in 1922, age 84.

Wanamaker's department store.

Washington Mews
The Namesake: Washington Square.

Formerly called Washington Alley, the Mews was the site of stables for the horses kept by Washington Square residents.

Washington Mews, looking east, 1905.

Washington Place
The Namesake: Washington Square.

The street abutting the square area was named in 1833, when the area was becoming fashionable.

Crowds outside Commodore Vanderbilt's residence, 10 Washington Place, on the morning of his death (January 7, 1877).

Washington Square
The Namesake: George Washington.

In the beginning a marshy place through which Minetta Brook gurgled, the square's site first was inhabited by Angolan blacks, freed by the Dutch in 1644 after they had spent almost two decades as slaves: they were alloted the land for farming. Later the area became a pauper's graveyard and the scene of public hangings. Converted into a parade ground for the militia in the 1820s, the square soon attracted fashionable neighbors—and New York University, which erected its initial building there in 1837. The Washington Square Memorial Arch, first built of wood, was put up in 1889 to commemorate the centennial of George Washington's inauguration as President. The idea was that of William Rhinelander Stewart, who lived at No. 17 Washington Square North. Reading that a parade to mark the occasion would march from the square up Fifth Avenue, he decided it must have an arch to march through. He promptly passed the hat among residents of Washington Square, Waverly Place and Fifth Avenue up to 14th Street, refusing money from anyone else. He raised $2,765, which proved to be $66.50 more than the arch cost. Stanford White designed the monument so successfully that popular demand insisted on its recreation in marble. Contributions poured in from all over the city and suburbs: Ignace Jan Paderewski gave a benefit at the Metropolitan Opera House that raised $4,500, and workmen who cut the marble in Tuckahoe chipped in $100. The completed arch, 73 feet 6 inches in total height and 47 feet 9 inches high at its opening, exceeded its $150,000 budget by $28,000. The arch was dedicated on April 30, 1895. The sculpture on the western pedestal, of a group in which Washington is the central figure, was executed and added in 1918 by A. Stirling Calder, father of Alexander Calder.

Water Street

The Namesake: the East River waters that washed the street at high tide in the 17th century.

When the first City Hall, known as the Stadt Huys, was established in a tavern building in 1653, rising water often swirled about its foundations and a retaining wall was built to protect them. Continued erosion elsewhere along the street forced residents to drive planks on end into the riverbank and in 1692 the city began a landfill program and sold the lots thus created. Front and South streets developed on the fill and Water Street, originally one block long, was extended.

Store at 160 Water Street, in 1836.

Washington Street

The Namesake: George Washington.

Land for the street was ceded to the city by Trinity Church in 1808.

Watts Street

The Namesake: John Watts, last City Recorder under British rule.

As an assemblyman, Watts protested the billeting of British soldiers on New York's citizens. He was a co-founder of the Leake and Watts Orphan Asylum and a monument to him stands in Trinity Churchyard.

Weehawken Street

The Namesake: Weehawken Market there, where produce from New Jersey was offered.

The market opened in 1834.

West Houston Street

(*See* Houston Street.)

Waverly Place

The Namesake: Sir Walter Scott's novel *Waverley*, published in 1814.

Scott had many admirers in Greenwich Village and the street was named by petition of the residents in 1833, a year after Scott's death.

London
MACMILLAN AND CO., LIMITED
NEW YORK : THE MACMILLAN COMPANY
1906

All rights reserved

West Broadway

The Namesake: Broadway. (West Broadway's name had the same motivation behind it as East Broadway's, to lessen Broadway's traffic congestion).

From Barclay Street to Reade Street, the thoroughfare appears on a 1767 map but is left nameless. By 1797 it was designated as Chapel Street and in 1831 the portion of it that runs from Barclay to Murray was renamed College Place. A decade later the segment from Murray Street to Canal Street was renamed West Broadway. It now extends to La Guardia Place, which formerly was part of West Broadway.

West End Avenue

The Namesake: the city's West End,
as it was called, which was gaining
prestige with the creation of Riverside Park.

Until 1880, the street was part of
Eleventh Avenue. The stretch from
72nd Street to 106th Street was renamed to make it sound classier.

West End Avenue at 75th Street, 1915.

West Street
The Namesake: its location.

In one form or another West Street seems to have existed as early as 1800, but it was officially laid out in 1830.

View of the docks from West Street, 1869.

Whitehall Street
The Namesake: London's Whitehall.

The street is the site of the governor's house built by Peter Stuyvesant, and when the British took over the city they christened the street and building for England's seat of government—no doubt with their tongues firmly in their cheeks.

Governor Stuyvesant's house, built in 1658, renamed "Whitehall" by the British.

W.H. Seward Park
The Namesake: William Henry Seward, Secretary of State in the cabinets of Abraham Lincoln and Andrew Johnson, 1861-1869.

Seward, who was born in the village of Florida, New York, in 1801 and lived most of his life in Auburn, New York, was New York State's Governor from 1839 to 1843. He was elected a U.S. Senator (by the legislature) in 1849. His greatest achievement as Secretary of State was the purchase of Alaska from Russia for $7.2 million—a deal dubbed at the time "Seward's Folly." He died in 1872.

William Henry Seward (seated, at left) signing the treaty for the purchase of Alaska.

Willett Street

The Namesake: Colonel Marinus Willett, a leading pre-Revolution radical, Revolutionary army officer, sheriff of New York (1784–88 and 1792–96) and mayor (1807). Originally a cabinetmaker, he grew rich as a merchant and became a prosperous landowner.

Two streets were named for Willett, but one—Sheriff Street, which ran south from Houston Street in the vicinity of Hamilton Fish Park—has been obliterated. Willett, once a student at King's College (now Columbia) and a veteran of the French and Indian War—he had been an 18-year-old lieutenant in Oliver de Lancey's regiment—became a fiery activist among the Sons of Liberty before the Revolution: twice in 1775 he participated in guerilla raids to capture British arms. In the war, he first served as a captain under Alexander McDougall (*see* MacDougal Street) and emerged as a colonel commended by Congress for bravery. Mayor James Duane (*see* Duane Street) named him sheriff at the first postwar meeting of the Common Council in 1784. As sheriff, he conducted a city census at a cost of £47. Between terms as sheriff, Willett, at President Washington's behest, negotiated a treaty with the Creek Indians. But he refused a commission as a brigadier general because he did not want to fight Indians, and returned to his post as sheriff. In 1807, he succeeded DeWitt Clinton as mayor. Willett died in 1830, age 90.

Colonel Marinus Willett.

William Street

The Namesake: Willem Beeckman (*see* Beekman Street).

Wooster Street

The Namesake: David Wooster, a lackluster Revolutionary general who was killed in action.

Wooster, who was born in Connecticut in 1711 and was graduated from Yale in 1738, had had thirty years of naval and military experience with Connecticut and English troops when the Revolution began, and the Connecticut Assembly in 1775 named him a major general commanding six regiments. At the request of New York, he led his Connecticut troops in the Battle of Harlem and the Battle of Long Island, whereupon Congress appointed him a brigadier general of the Continental Army—a rank that Wooster considered beneath him. The truth was that while Wooster was adored by his undisciplined soldiers, he was considered inept by his fellow officers, including General Washington. Wooster died in a brief battle with the British at Ridgefield, Connecticut, on April 17, 1777, and Congress voted to erect a monument to him, but never built it. But Wooster had organized an early lodge of Free Masons in New Haven in 1750, and Free Masons put up a monument to his memory in Danbury in 1854.

General David Wooster.

York Avenue

The Namesake: Sergeant Alvin C. York, a one-time conscientious objector and reluctant warrior who became the nation's greatest hero of World War I: singlehandedly, he silenced 35 German machine guns, killed 25 enemy soldiers and took 132 prisoners in the Meuse-Argonne offensive on October 8, 1918.

A six-foot, 200-pound Tennessee mountaineer who abjured liquor, gambling and profanity and who fought the draft on religious grounds, York went into the army determined "to do the best I could." He emerged from the service with the Medal of Honor and almost fifty other decorations. When he returned from France in May 1919, New York gave him a tumultuous reception and the New York Stock Exchange suspended operations while brokers carried him around the floor on their shoulders. But York went back to the Tennessee hills, refusing lecture tours and acting roles on the ground that "this uniform ain't for sale." When a 1941 movie, in which Gary Cooper played York, earned rich royalties for the ex-soldier, he used the money to establish a school for mountain children. He died in 1964, at age 76, a farmer, hunter and modern frontiersman until illness felled him. York Avenue had been named for him long before, in 1928.

Worth Street

The Namesake: William Jenkins Worth, a major-general reputed to have been the first American soldier to enter Mexico City in the war with Mexico in 1848.

Worth, a store clerk in Hudson, N.Y., and Albany, joined the army in the War of 1812, in which he was so seriously wounded that he was not expected to live. He remained in the service and, though not a West Pointer, commanded the U.S. Military Academy from 1820 to 1828. A brave and able soldier, he was personally so egotistical, truculent and insulting that his superior, General Winfield Scott, once had to place him under arrest. Worth died of cholera in 1849 while in command of Texas, and is buried in Madison Square. The monument to him there is his tombstone.

Major General William Jenkins Worth.

York Street

The Namesake: undetermined.

York Street was part of Hubert Street until 1823.

Sergeant Alvin York.

Picture Credits

Cover
Library of Congress

Introduction
Page 6: Library of Congress
Page 7: NY Public Library Picture
    Collection
Page 8-9: NY Public Library, Picture Collection
Page 10: NY Public Library, Picture Collection
Page 11: NY Public Library, Picture
    Collection

Adam Clayton Powell Jr. Blvd.
Compix, UPI

Admiral George Dewey Promenade
Photo by Frances Benjamin Johnston,
Library of Congress

Albany Street
New-York Historical Society

Allen Street
New-York Historical Society

A. Philip Randolph Square
Wide World

Astor Place
NY Public Library, Picture Collection

Audubon Avenue
Courtesy of The White House Collection

Avenue of the Americas
NY Daily News

Bank Street
Museum of the City of NY

Barclay Street
NY Public Library, Picture Collection

Battery Place
NY Public Library, Picture Collection

Baxter Street
Library of Congress

Beach Street
Library of Congress

Beaver Street
NY Public Library, Picture Collection

Beekman Place
Museum of the City of NY

Bennett Avenue
Library of Congress

Benson Street
New-York Historical Society

Bethune Street
Courtesy of Graham-Windham Services to
Families & Children, and of the Frick Art
Reference Library

Bleecker Street
NY Public Library, Picture Collection

Bogardus Place
NY Public Library, Picture Collection

Bowery
Library of Congress

Bowling Green
Library of Congress

Bridge Street
Museum of the City of NY

Broadway
Library of Congress

Broome Street
Library of Congress

Burling Slip
New-York Historical Society

Canal Street
Museum of the City of NY

Cardinal Hayes Place
NY Daily News

Carl Schurz Park (2)
Library of Congress

Cathedral Parkway
Museum of the City of NY

Cedar Street
New York Public Library, Picture
Collection

Central Park West
Frank Leslie's Illustrated Newspaper,
September 7, 1889

Centre Street
Museum of the City of NY

Chatham Square
Library of Congress

Cherokee Place
William E. Sauro, The New York Times

Chrystie Street
New-York Historical Society

Claremont Avenue
Museum of the City of NY

Clinton Street
NY Public Library, Picture Collection

Coenties Slip & Alley
NY Public Library, Picture Collection

Columbus Avenue
NY Public Library, Picture Collection

Columbus Circle
Library of Congress

Cooper Square
Library of Congress

Cortlandt Street
New-York Historical Society

Crosby Street
Museum of the City of NY

Delancey Street
NY Public Library, Picture Collection

Depew Place
Museum of the City of NY

Depeyster Street
Library of Congress

Dongan Place
NY Public Library, Picture Collection

Duane Street
Museum of the City of NY

Duke Ellington Boulevard (2)
Frank Driggs Collection

Dyckman Street
Museum of the City of NY

East River Drive
NY Daily News

Edgecombe Avenue
Museum of the City of NY

Elk Street
Library of Congress

Ericsson Place
NY Public Library, Picture Collection

Exchange Place and Exchange Alley
New-York Historical Society

Father Demo Square
Edward Hausner, The New York Times

Fifth Avenue
NY Public Library, Picture Collection

Finn Square
United Press International

Foley Square
Museum of the City of NY

Fort Tryon
New-York Historical Society

Fort Washington Avenue
Courtesy of the U.S. Naval Academy
Museum

Franklin Square
Museum of the City of NY

Franklin Street and Franklin Place
Library of Congress

Frederick Douglass Circle
Library of Congress

Freedom Place
Declan Haun, Black Star

Fulton Street
Photo by Ed Spiro, courtesy of
Cooper-Hewitt Museum

Gold Street
NY Public Library, Picture Collection

Gracie Square
Courtesy of NY Convention and Visitors Bureau

Gramercy Park
Museum of the City of NY

Greene Street
Library of Congress

Grove Street, Grove Court
Museum of the City of NY

Hamilton Fish Park
Library of Congress

Hamilton Place and Hamilton Terrace
New-York Historical Society

Hammarskjold Plaza
Courtesy of United Nations

Hancock Place and Hancock Square
NY Public Library, Picture Collection

Harlem River Drive
Museum of the City of NY

Harry Howard Square
Museum of the City of NY, Davies Coll.

Henderson Place
Museum of the City of NY

Henry Hudson Parkway
Library of Congress

Henry Street
Museum of the City of NY,
Wurts Brothers Coll.

Herald Square
Museum of the City of NY

Horatio Street
Library of Congress

Houston Street
Library of Congress

Hubert Street
Museum of the City of NY

Indian Road
NY Public Library, Picture Collection

Irving Place
Museum of the City of NY

Jackson Street
Library of Congress

James J. Walker Park
Museum of the City of NY

Jefferson Street
Library of Congress

John Street
Museum of the City of NY

Jumel Place and Jumel Terrace
New-York Historical Society

Kingsbridge Avenue
Library of Congress

Lafayette Street
Library of Congress

Laurel Hill Terrace
NY Public Library, Picture Collection

Lenox Avenue
Museum of the City of NY

Leroy Street
Library of Congress

Lexington Avenue
Library of Congress

Liberty Street
NY Public Library, Picture Collection

Lillian Wald Drive
Library of Congress

Ludlow Street
NY Public Library, Picture Collection

MacDougal Street and MacDougal Alley
New-York Historical Society

Macombs Place
Museum of the City of NY

Madison Avenue
Library of Congress

Madison Square
Library of Congress

Magaw Place
New-York Historical Society

Maiden Lane
New-York Historical Society

Mangin Street
New-York Historical Society

Marcus Garvey Park
Compix, UPI

Margaret Corbin Drive
New-York Historical Society

Milligan Place
Museum of the City of NY

Mitchell Place
New-York Historical Society

Mitchell Square
New-York Historical Society

Monroe Street
Library of Congress

Montgomery Street
New-York Historical Society

Morton Street
New-York Historical Society

Mott Street
New-York Historical Society

Nassau Street
NY Public Library, Picture Collection

New Street
Museum of the City of NY

North Moore Street
Museum of the City of NY

Orchard Street
Museum of the City of NY,
Byron Coll.

Park Avenue
Courtesy of NY Convention &
Visitors Bureau

Park Place and Park Row
NY Public Library, Picture Collection

Patchin Place
Library of Congress

Pearl Street
NY Public Library, Picture Collection

Peck Slip
Museum of the City of NY

Perry Street
Library of Congress

Pershing Square
Library of Congress

Pike Street, Pike Slip
Library of Congress

Pleasant Avenue
Museum of the City of NY

Rector Street
Library of Congress

Renwick Street
New-York Historical Society

Riverside Drive
Harper's Weekly, July 17, 1886

Rivington Street
New-York Historical Society

Robert F. Wagner Sr. Place
Museum of the City of NY

Rockefeller Plaza
Library of Congress

Roosevelt Square
Library of Congress

Rose Street
Library of Congress

Rutgers Street and Rutgers Slip
New-York Historical Society

St. James Place
Museum of the City of NY

St. John's Lane
NY Public Library, Picture Collection

St. Nicholas Avenue
Museum of the City of NY

Sara Roosevelt Parkway
Franklin D. Roosevelt Library, Hyde Park

Schiff Parkway
Library of Congress

Sheridan Square
Library of Congress

Sherman Square
Library of Congress

Sniffen Court
Jack Manning, The New York Times

South Street
Museum of the City of NY

South William Street
Museum of the City of NY

Spruce Street
NY Public Library, Picture Collection

Staple Street
NY Public Library, Picture Collection

Straus Park
Photo by Marion Bernstein

Stuyvesant Square
Museum of the City of NY

Sutton Place and Sutton Square
Minnesota Historical Society

Szold Place
Culver Pictures

Theatre Alley
New-York Historical Society

Tiemann Place
Museum of the City of NY

Times Square
Culver Pictures

Trimble Place
Museum of the City of NY

Union Square
Museum of the City of NY

United Nations Plaza
Courtesy of NY Convention &
Visitors Bureau

Vanderbilt Avenue
Museum of the City of NY

Vesey Street
Museum of the City of NY

Wadsworth Avenue
Library of Congress

Wall Street
Courtesy of D. Graham

Wanamaker Place
Museum of the City of NY

Washington Mews
New-York Historical Society

Washington Place
Museum of the City of NY

Washington Square
Museum of City of NY

Water Street
New-York Historical Society

Waverly Place
Courtesy of R. L. Eakins

West End Avenue
Museum of the City of NY,
Wurts Brothers Coll.

West Street
Museum of the City of NY

Whitehall Street
NY Public Library, Picture Collection

W. H. Seward Park
Library of Congress

Willett Street
Museum of the City of NY

Wooster Street
Library of Congress

Worth Street
Library of Congress

York Avenue
Brown Brothers

Appendix

Henry Moscow

A veteran newspaper and magazine editor and the author or co-author of numerous books, Henry Moscow has cherished a life-long love affair with his native New York City. He has published works on subjects as diverse as gardening and psychology, but his major interest is history. In this book, he focuses that interest on the object of his affection.

Acknowledgements

I am deeply grateful to Helen Rose Cline, the now retired Parish Recorder of the Parish of Trinity Church of the City of New York, for unearthing the namesakes of streets related to the church; Phyllis Barr, consultant for archival management to Trinity Parish; Frank Stankus of *The New York Times* for providing biographical data on a number of individuals; and Morton B. Lawrence of *Park East,* Ruth Jimenez, formerly of *Life,* and Charles P. Sniffen III for offering clues in a couple of elusive cases. I owe sincere thanks too to the everhelpful staffs of the New York Public Library's local history room, map room and newspaper annex; and of the Mercantile Library, the American Irish Historical Society and the New York Historical Society. My thanks also to the staffs of the Cooper Union Library; the Nyack Public Library; the Finkelstein Memorial Library, Spring Valley, New York; and the Library of the Performing Arts; New York Public Library at Lincoln Center. I have availed also of the facilities of the Municipal Reference Library, the New York City Central Archives, and the files of Manhattan Surrogate's Court.

Henry Moscow

Special thanks

Special thanks are due for the expert and generous help offered to the picture researchers by Wendy Shadwell, Curator of Prints, The New York Historical Society; by A.K. Baragwanath, Senior Curator, and Esther Brumberg, Photo Librarian, The Museum of the City of New York; by Lois Elias, Public Relations Manager, New York Convention & Visitors Bureau

DATE DUE	
APR 0 9 2002	
APR 0 9 2002	
OCT 3 1 2003	